Wicca 334
Further Advanced Topics in Wiccan Belief

Wicca 334
Further Advanced Topics in Wiccan Belief
Part Two of a Master Class in Wicca

Kaatryn MacMorgan-Douglas
With Llysse Smith Wylle

ᵂℒ𝔪
𝔵

COVENSTEAD PRESS   BUFFALO, NEW YORK

Wicca 334: Advanced Topics in Wiccan Belief
ISBN: 978-0-6151-7536-2

Books by Kaatryn MacMorgan-Douglas:
All One Wicca (Fall 2001, Fall 2007)

A Master Class in Wicca:
        Wicca 333 (Spring 2003, October 2007)
        Wicca 334: (December 2007)

The Ethical Eclectic (July 2007)
The Circle, Cubed (May 2008)

This work is dedicated to anyone who ever read a patently false book on Wicca and discovered that it was false… and rather than deciding to write off Wicca as a whole because of the experience, went looking for the "more" that is out there.

…and also, *all* my work is dedicated to my family, especially Phoenix, who tries to keep me from writing like King Friday XIII, whom I have the momentous and apparently genetic misfortune of recurrently resembling in my verbal interactions.

Contents

Introduction:

This work is the follow up to *Wicca 333: Advanced Topics in Wiccan Belief*, my first foray into the world of "advanced Wicca." I am unsure about how comfortable I feel with the idea of separating the teaching of Wicca into beginning and advanced Wicca. *Wicca 333 certainly* addressed topics that a newbie would be unfamiliar with, but it wasn't advanced in the same way Calculus III is advanced over Calculus I. I have never been comfortable with the idea that there must be some kind of arbiter of "the next level" or that someone must determine "what is truly advanced." It's true that I'm weary of beginning material on Wicca—and with the exception of the further revised *All One Wicca*, I will probably never provide beginning material again (unless someone pitches me a really good proposal). However, I don't really see what is provided in this book as something beyond the average Wiccan's ken.

I label these topics "advanced" because they are the types of issues that Wiccans discuss and find that newcomers to Wicca react to by saying, "I'd never thought of that before." In addition, the topics are presented with the assumption that you have a familiarity with the basic concepts that allows me to avoid restating them. If these topics are "advanced" it is only because my friends and family are, and I've written this work as much for them as for anyone.

Wicca 334 is the first thing I've ever written that doesn't stand alone as a work. In fact, this book is a continuation of *Wicca 333*, and the topics are numbered to reflect that. It assumes you have read *333*, including its rather extensive introduction explaining the format of the book, my pedagogical foci and the like. Many of the chapters are shorter than those in *Wicca 333* because there are many things defined in *Wicca 333* mentioned here in passing—things that I hammered hard on in *333* and think you probably get by now. Those shorter chapters do make this a slimmer volume and a faster read, but I felt that a more concise tome would be better appreciated by my readers.

That being said, I don't think you'll be lost reading this alone, but I do think that it may be confusing to people who don't realize that it is a sequel. For the record, however—and to be utterly clear—this is a *further* collection of advanced topics, not a collection of topics that are "further advanced." It is an imperfect subtitle, but better than the alternative titles we proposed-*Wicca 334: Did you think of this? Wicca 334: I left something out. Wicca 334: You asked for it. Wicca 334: I'm never finished with anything, why stop here?*

Collectively, both *Wicca 333* and *Wicca 334* are known as *A Master Class in Wicca*. I am aware that not everyone is familiar with the term master class. It refers to a seminar, usually quite small, in which a person thoroughly schooled in a topic teaches and works with a group of students who are also thoroughly schooled in a topic. For me, the term master class recalls the drama, music and public speaking classes I attended in which the lecturer hand picked his students and worked with their individual strengths and weaknesses. As many of my readers know, 333 and 334 are collaborative efforts in many ways. My students, friends and family had a large amount of input into what I discussed. There is not a single topic in either book that wasn't suggested by a student — it is for them that this book is designed.

As in the previous work, many of the topics, aren't about Wicca *per se*, but instead are about issues that are of interest to Wiccans or are important to the study of Wicca. They may either be issues that the Wiccan community deals with regularly or that are of interest to those who study our religion in the broader light of comparative theology. There is a rather obtuse idea pervasive in the Wiccan community: that the study of Wicca should encompass *only* the writings of Wiccan authors, which are about Wiccan ritual. This is an incredibly silly idea, in part because you could study all the books on Wicca ever written at this point within a couple of years (something I think no one would find amusing, as the level of redundancy is extreme) and in part because Wicca neither developed nor progressed within a vacuum. To understand Wicca, to really get it at a deep level, you have to look both at it and around it — study both Wicca and those things that touch upon it.

By request, Appendix A of this work includes another self-test, an extension of the material in Appendix C of *Wicca 333*, which I was surprised to find people enjoyed immensely. Taken together, they provide 100 questions on Wicca, more than enough of a test for anyone. As I said in *333*:

This is not a test of Witchy-ness, nor is it a test of proficiency in Wicca. It represents topics that intermediate to advanced students should've been exposed to, even to a slight degree. If you glance through it and find you have no idea what any of these things are, it might indicate that the material herein will be beyond your depth. If you read through it and are familiar with all the concepts, you may find parts of this book below your level of expertise. If you find yourself in the middle, you're probably smack dab in the center of the target audience.

I do not think it likely there will be a Wicca 335 unless some brave coauthor selects the topics. Picking out 12 topics from the many suggestions was like pulling teeth and made my family miserable, as I went around endlessly asking "which do you think is a better topic?" as I presented them with a list of prospectives that they often had no ideas about at all. My short monograph *The Ethical Eclectic* had actually been in the works since before I began writing this, and goes in a completely different direction while covering a lot of the same bases. This book is for Wiccans; that one for Eclectic Pagans of all sorts.

With my own students, I have addressed applying a format similar to this to a few works on ritual construction, but even the creation of small books like this one and *333* require an inordinate amount of time… and I would not wish to create something less than twenty or thirty people would wish to read. As always, if you think that something I've proposed sounds interesting to you, personally, feel free to contact me at Kaatryn@MacMorgan.org and suggest I work on it. Like any teacher who finds teaching fun, I can generally be convinced to put my willpower behind something if enough students feel a need for it. As many people know, this brief series got its start when advanced students of my own bemoaned the lack of advanced material and became a series when their reaction to *333* was clamoring for more. I'm always willing to listen to what people want, so long as it doesn't violate my ethical principles or seem to be out of my areas of knowledge. I don't always understand *why* people want it — the sales of *All One Wicca* outside the UEW community still confuse me — but if enough people speak out, I'll acknowledge that they *do* want it.

Don't get me wrong. I love this book. It was often fun to write and a joy to research. It is exactly what I would've liked to find on the shelves of my library once I'd reached the advanced student level. I am just unconvinced the world is prepared for *even more* advanced topics, or that the master class warrants another semester.

So, by all means, enjoy this one,

Kaatryn MacMorgan-Douglas

Topic Thirteen: The Lord and Lady Do Not Comprise Their Own Pantheon.

Are the Wiccan "Lord and Lady" standalone gods that do not have any relevance to a culture? How did this idea develop? Are there names for the gods? Many names? One name? Is this another version of "all gods are one God?" How does Modern Wicca answer the problem of names for the gods?

The Names of the Gods in Early Modern Wicca[1]

Early Modern Wicca, as practiced by Gardner, borrowed many things from the spiritual movements around it. The Masons, British Spiritualists, Egyptologists, Crowley and the Theosophical Society all left distinct imprints on Early Modern Wicca. Gardner's love of archaic weapons and naturalism were even translated into this nascent religion. It may well be that Gardner really thought he was reconstructing an ancient religion, and that these things were transported into Wicca because he felt they had found their way into the sources around him through this ancient religion. Without the presence of some form of extensive recording of his thoughts, we just can't know.

There is a trend in Modernism to paint Gardner as a bit of a P.T. Barnum and write off everything he did as an attempt to pawn off to people this fake religion. My very first formal study of anything was of acting, and method acting at that, so I certainly understand the need to try to grasp a historic figure's motivation. I can see how a person might choose to portray Gardner as a salesman of shoddy merchandise, but I'm just not sure that is an accurate portrayal. It may well be that he believed what he was teaching — not just that he conned his students into believing that he believed it. The true scholar has to try to remain neutral about it.

Your stance toward Early Modern Wicca can flavor how you see Gardner; it is perhaps because of my hard Modernism that I really don't personally care what his motivations were. I am focused on the now and on actual history as an understanding of

---

[1] Throughout *Wicca 334*, we will use the terms given in the timeline presented in *Wicca 333*. It is highly recommended you understand these distinctions, as they are vital to any coherent discussion of Wicca in this format.

the now. This leads to an interest in *the idea* of Wicca as an ancient religion, without too much of a focus on why it was first taught like that. For the purpose of this work, I shall be neither Gardner's apologist nor his accuser. He taught that Wicca was the modern remnants of an ancient great religion. There is no true evidence of what he taught, and I don't care whether he was outright lying or just mistaken. I'm not sure you should, either.

That caveat being thrown out there, we can now discuss Early Modern Wicca without prejudice. It is a common claim, both from the *all-gods-are-one* crowd and the *names-of-the gods-don't-matter* crowd, that the reason Wiccans describe the gods in the terms of Lord and Lady and regularly do not name the gods beyond that is because, as with Modern and Post-Modern Wiccans, Early Modern Wiccans viewed the names of the gods as UPG[2], experienced differently by all Wiccans. Thus in using the generic, Early Modern Wiccans were affirming the differences in individual beliefs.

The only problem with this lovely belief is that it isn't true. The Lord and the Lady in Early Modern Wicca had names; they just were names restricted to those of the inner circle, names revealed in a mystery rite. As I discussed in Topic Five, the fact that these names are commonly revealed only to those of an inner circle is often given as a reason why so few understand this concept. I'm unsure I agree with that assessment, being the sort of person who generally thinks the best of people until they prove otherwise.

The idea in Early Modern Wicca is that names have power. The names you are known by, the true names of the gods and the names you are given by your brethren all exhibit different levels of power and therefore should not be shared with people incapable of using that power… or immoral enough to abuse it. In part, this is why the names of the gods are generally oath-bound; it's an oath that few are willing to break. The names are kept secret because they have power. What is important to understand is that they did exist in Early Modern Wicca. You got to a point where you were introduced to Freya and Pan[3], or what-

---

[2] Unverified Personal Gnosis, discussed ad nauseum in 333.
[3] These were the names used in some EMW groups. I find these names particularly problematic, and don't personally suggest using them.

ever the names of the gods in your coven or tradition were. Your UPG was unimportant, because you followed the same god as the next member of your coven. If you studied long and hard, you discovered that the Lord and Lady had names. Just as they knew your secret name among the Wicca, so you learned theirs.

To make this painfully clear, imagine our intrepid Wiccan Caitlin has just joined the Coven of the Fifth Grail, a coven based on British Traditional Witchcraft. Caitlin spends her first year learning the most basic of stuff—what the coven rules are, the meaning of the coven's name and other introductory materials. Her coven, being of the stricter kind, doesn't allow her to attend most of the high holy rites in this first year, but she learns a bit about them—when they are, why that calendar is used and things like that.

After a year and a day of satisfactory performance, Caitlin is initiated. She is given an eke name, and formally introduced to the leaders of the group and the gods. Even at this point, they are still just "The Lord and Lady," but she is introduced to them by her new name and as a full member of the group. Even the Priest and Priestess, who Caitlin knows, are reintroduced to her in their full roles. She even learns some more basic stuff about the group, usually including some sort of foundational myth.

In the next one to two years, Caitlin learns more about the structure of the Wheel of the Year, why the group meets when it does, and learns how to construct ritual. More foundational mythology follows, and after two or more years have passed, Caitlin is introduced to the inner court of the group. She is now one of the caretakers of the knowledge she herself has received. It is only at this point she learns the names of the gods of her coven— in this example Diana and Pan—names she is forbidden to speak aloud where any of those outside the inner circle can hear. (The "forbidden to speak" part would be in the context of religion. She could discuss, say, Lady Diana, or Diana Ross... or while cooking she could ask "Could you hand me that pan?" Perhaps she could even discuss Diana and Pan as deities in other cultures, just not as *her* deities.)

If it is her wish to become a priestess, it is at this point Caitlin begins that training. She is now, after a minimum of two years, a full Wiccan in this group. Only at that point does she know for sure that the Lord and Lady have names, and what those names are.

How did "No Names" come to be?

The names of the gods are part of a grand body of material not available to mere initiates, called the "inner court-" or "inner circle-" knowledge. Since one of the core beliefs in Wicca is that names have power, bestowing and learning names was seen by Early Modern Wiccan groups as an act of power. To gain this power, you had to prove yourself, primarily by moving through the ranks of your coven or tradition. You had to demonstrate trustworthiness, knowledge and reliability, at the least.

The problem is that many people don't stick with covens, even good ones. In my experience, about ten percent of my direct students go on to the highest level of study. Another thirty-five percent or so go up to the level just below that. Based on numerous conversations with members of other traditions and other members of my own, UEW is above average in that percentage, and I'm above average in retention for UEW.

Based on discussions with other groups and the experiences of friends and family, if you take a coven of twelve in an established tradition, two or three will go on to the middle level(s) and about half the time, one of those few will continue on in your coven without changing traditions or founding a new tradition. The rest either leave Wicca entirely, switch to new covens or found their own traditions, regardless of how little they've studied. This works out to a less than five percent chance that a person will continue in any established tradition. The retention rate is obviously higher in those traditions in which the status of being a member of the innermost circle is given without any work, or traditions which are the "only church on the street." There are some trads that have difficult inner circle work but still have high levels of retention because there are techniques that can improve retention (such as being selective about who you allow in your initial degree or who you'll teach)... but this five percent number is good, parsimonious and generally workable, so I'll stick with it.

With this number, the percentage of people trained in Early Modern Wicca who went on to learn the names of the gods is understandably low. It is likely, then, since Early Modern Wicca revealed the names of the gods at the inner circle but did not reveal the nature of that revelation before the moment of revelation itself, that people who left these earlier traditions before ascending to the inner circle simply never learned that the gods had names. It is reasonable to guess many of them assumed the reason that the gods were unnamed was simply because they had no names — probably the simplest explanation of that perceived fact, and way more comfortable than the belief that one is missing knowledge.

This makes a lot of sense when you understand the Abrahamic view of the power of the name of god. In that worldview, god's proper name is not only reserved for the use of god alone, but is so powerful that merely writing it can be an act of intense magic coupled with a healthy dose of hubris. In that world view, god is just "God" because to speak his name, even if you knew it, would be a supreme act that separated you from humanity. Depending on the Abrahamic mythos you were using, this name could destroy you outright or even destroy the creation itself.

The problem here is that the name of the gods in Wicca is related to, and reflective of, the secret names of the individual Wiccan (covered in the next topic) in a coven. As you progress through the levels, (or degrees, circles, initiations, mysteries, ranks) you learn names that bring you closer and closer to the final name of divinity, or even the revelation of the all. The gods have names, but to even admit that fact is, in some traditions, a violation of one's oath. Therefore the half-trained Wiccan, especially the one that leaves a tradition in a huff assuming he knows it all, not only does not know the names of the gods but does not know the gods have names.

As cynical and awful as it is to say, I am beginning to believe that the reason that people make this mistake is because their own teachers claim to have a knowledge of the original core theology of Wicca that they just don't have. In other words, it seems horrible but likely that the teaching that the gods have no name is nothing more or less than an attempt to cover up the fact that many Wiccan traditions are based on imperfect understandings of the traditions that spawned them.

To make this clear, let's imagine another member of the imaginary Coven of the Fifth Grail. For the sake of argument, we'll call this one Patrick. (I think, in general, all the Joes and Freds and Caitlins in the world have been abused enough and need some space.) Patrick joins at the same time as Caitlin, and spends the first year and a day the same way she did—learning the basic coven's introductory material. By the middle of his second year, however, he's starting to chafe at the group's rules and is picking up books on Wicca and information on other groups on the sly. Patrick is, in fact, a Tradition Track Wiccan, something we'll get to later.

He decides he's had enough and leaves the group after his second year. He feels, with the combination of his book knowledge, initiation and participation in a few rituals, he knows all there is to know, including the story of The Lord and Lady, gods with no names. They *have* to have no names, he figures, because no one has mentioned a name near him, and he's kept an ear out for hints that they have a name and other hidden facts.

In an ideal parting, the coven would provide him with some form of exit interview, in which he would learn, at the least, what he has gotten wrong about the tradition. Patrick, however, decides he's used the coven as long as he's needed to and burns his bridges fast, putting the coven in the uncomfortable position as the source of some of his misinformation, as well as his information. The coven can only hope that when he gets things wrong he doesn't lay the blame on them.

How did the Idea of Many Names come to be?

We see the idea of many names or of divine patronage—that one can only follow the deity that appears to be invested in your well being or who you are in contact with (Patron deities)—in traditions that can trace their roots cleanly to older forms of Wicca. These traditions aren't necessarily lineaged, meaning that their founders or their founders' teachers taught by Gardner, but many can still show where, when and how they are related to older forms of Wicca. They can show their theological lineage. The fact that these divergent traditions share the "many names" concept speaks to something highly functional within the concept itself, or at least its availability.

Unlike the idea of no names, the idea of many names is something that exists in the literature that created Early Modern Wicca and was created by it. We see the idea in Valiente's

Charge of the Goddess[4], although a case can be made (and was, earlier) that she is, in fact, referring to the mythological she-of-many-names of Dianic Paganism and Murrayite "anthropology." We see it in the study of IE mythological trends expected of most so-called British Traditional Witchcraft traditions, and we see the bastard stepchild of that study on occasion, too: they're the people who claim to teach a Proto-Indo-European faith that they've reverse engineered from the faiths of the past four thousand years (or claim to have experienced in a past life... but that's another thing altogether).

"Many names" and "all names" have distinct differences in Indo-European cultures. No gods claimed to have all names, but most gods regularly had many names. Hades, for example, whose name means "the unseen," is also called the "many-greeter" (my favorite epithet of Hades—makes you think twice about the smiling old folks in front of Wal-Mart, huh?), "the wealthy," or "guardian of great treasures." When you add to such knowledge an understanding that the Romans generally (but not always) saw the difference between their co-opted gods and the indigenous form of those same gods as a difference in epithet, not in deity, you can sort of understand the idea that one god may have many faces which he shows to different peoples. Just as I, mere mortal that I am, am known as Kaatryn@ to my mail server, Hun to my wife, Mommy to my son and Ms. MacMorgan to people I've just met, so the gods, we are told, have different names for different peoples at different times.

This is different from the idea that a singular god or goddess is *all* the gods and goddesses. She-Of-Many-Names, for example, may be Diana and Artemis. If you believe that the deity the Greeks and Romans called Diana and Artemis is, in fact, a sort of Proto-Indo-European supergoddess, she might be Ishtar, Astoreth and Inanna as well. What she is not, even in this flawed view, is the same goddess as another in her pantheon: Diana may be Artemis, but she's not Hera.

In fact, Valiente's Proto-Indo-European super-goddess of her Charge lists the names of *two* distinct goddess subtypes, both of them falling under the subtype of "maiden deities." The warrior

---

[4] Which has more to do, by far, with The Golden Ass than anything else.

maiden, chaste and virginal (embodied in Artemis/Diana,) and the sacred whore, familiar to us perhaps most obviously as Aphrodite. This seems, at first, as if this goddess, who we call She-Of-Many-Names or just Somn[5], is two distinct deities bundled incoherently together until you remember that other bit of Wiccan mythology: the goddess who changes form from maiden to whore, or (in less loaded terms) from the sexual nonentity to the sexual entity.

This goddess is the divine interpretation of the rite portrayed on the frescos of The Villa of the Mysteries. As you no doubt know, these frescos were critical in Gardner's development of the Wiccan initiation ritual. (If you prefer a less modernist approach, they bear an amazing similarity to the rites Gardner practiced, in what must be one of the most extreme coincidences of all time.) This goddess, Somn, goes from the sexually naive but strong virginal figure to someone who must lose power in the initiation rite and regain it as a sexual entity.

Therefore the names used in Valiente's charge represent the many names of two goddesses that represent two stages in a woman's position in the coven. She is not the maiden, mother and crone—that interpretation comes later and enters Wicca through Dianic Paganism—but instead she is the representation of the two acceptable sexual entities in a fertility religion whose rites focus on the act, not the results. She is the never plucked fruit and the seasoned pro... or if you prefer, the initiate and the initiator.

Most literal polytheists, of course, shun this idea. For them, to claim that Artemis is Aphrodite is just a reflection of a bad understanding of mythology. Even then, note the lack of true mother goddesses in Somn. She is not a mother but a could-be mother. She has the power of sexual energy without all the uncomfortable ramifications of motherhood. She's daughter running wild in the woods, and the mistress running wild in the sheets... but never the jealous wife or the one asking a man how the bills will be paid.

This dichotomy, the innocent whore, is a thoroughly British phenomenon that fascinates us to this day and clearly fascinated

---

[5] I first heard She-Of-Many-Names called "Somn" in the early 1990s, and I am a fan of the name, personally.

Gardner. We see it in Lady Diana (who was, conveniently, named Diana); we see it in history, with the young Queen Elizabeth; we see it in the "colonies" with everyone from Eva Peron to Britney Spears. To quote Andrew Lloyd Webber (twice in two books) she's "a cross between a fantasy of the bedroom and a saint." Is it any wonder, then, that most of Wicca's earliest proponents were men? Or that Gardner "discovered" laws that favored younger and prettier priestesses? I think not! Somn is a male fantasy of female power and that is why she did not survive Early Modern Wicca without changing dramatically. Note that the only liturgical uses of the "many names" for the male deity were charges of the god that came late in the game and mirrored Valiente's charge. There is no He-Of-Many-Names in Early Modern Wicca; there is just the entity of male sexual prowess.

We Return, Grudgingly, to all gods are One God

We can now look at the issue of all gods being one (discussed in Topic Two) with renewed vigor. Not only were all gods not one in Early Modern Wicca, but the gods that *were* focused upon represented a sort of universal PIE pantheon reinterpreted through the classically educated English eye. The initiation rite, based on The Villa of the Mysteries, gets toned down to a sort of silk-tie kinkiness that would be scolded by Christian society, if discovered... but not rejected outright, as something more overtly religious might be.

With that in mind, we have to ask ourselves if Gardner would even recognize the ecstatic-deconstructionists for whom the practice of modern Wicca is about reverence for deity, and for whom the actual rituals of the religion are of secondary importance when compared to a vibrant relationship with the divine. It can certainly be argued that those practicing Wicca as "genuine religion" rather than as "flashy lifestyle" are very different from the Gardner's contemporaries in the early days. Anyone who has studied under the quiet, wise priest or priestess knows there is a huge and tangible difference between their practice and the practices of "media witches." As Gardner himself can be argued to have been a "media witch"—perhaps the ultimate, even in his own estimation (after all, Gardner claims to have exposed a religion that its practitioners had kept secret for centuries)—some may wonder if it's possible that he was also seeking something besides religion. We will never know for sure, and I'm not sure we'd want to.

One friend insists that the fact that the names of the deity are not important, or are of such little importance that they vary from early tradition to early tradition, is *not* a result of half-trained Wiccans running off to form new groups, as I mostly believe it is. Instead, he believes Early Modern Wicca was about finding a justification for sexual titillation that could withstand Christian skepticism. He points to the soft-core pulp porn of the day, which regularly portrayed innocent sweet things going crazy in so-called "heathen" rites where they lost their virginity and came out as hardened hellcats. Wicca's technical similarity to some parts of these stories, precursors of modern erotica, is not hard to see: the scourge, the knife, the cup... even the focus upon strange initiations in which the participants are clad either in velvet robes or nothing at all.

These pulp porn paperbacks followed a very familiar pattern of initiate and initiator. The sweet and innocent being is led into decadence and freedom from moral constraints after meeting the stranger who introduces him/her to a new way of thinking. These books challenge, much as the mere existence of non-Christian religion does, the very idea of society's having a common, innate morality. The initiate in these novels learns a truth normally forbidden to them by society, church and family. This is the same claim made by Early Modern Wicca, even if it's not the same truth.

A new religion teaching that living a secret life is the best defense to a Christian morality that will inevitably persecute you, my skeptical friend points out, makes religious experimentation with societal taboos not merely possible, but also consistent and logical. Indeed, this perspective assumes that sexual repression is the result of wicked Christians with their witch-trials and inquisitors. In his mindset, all gods are not one God because of some high-minded, Dion-Fortune-flavored pseudouniversalism, but instead because *which god* is worshipped is unimportant compared to the ecstatic experience of (sexual) communion with the divine.

As intriguing as his idea seems in some ways, it just doesn't have the ring of truth to me. It is correct that Wicca changed dramatically as free love and freer love became socially possible, if not acceptable. It is correct as well that if my friend's "sexual liberator hypothesis" were true we *would* see Wicca undergo a dramatic sea change from the mid 1950s to the late 1960s—a change that did in fact occur. Even so, it is more likely, in my opinion, that Gardner and his cohorts had genuine religious beliefs that also (and in some measure) elicited or revealed the choice to accept one's innate sexuality, especially in the context of the 1960s, rather than that they had overpowering sexual identities that required such a change in religious beliefs.

Had Wicca been created merely for its value as a sexual liberator, it's highly unlikely that there would be groups in which sexual experimentation did not exist. However the truth is that many if not most groups have little or nothing to do with sexual experimentation as a part of the religious experience. If, at its core, Wicca was created merely as a sexual liberator, instead we would see many, many groups based on the sexuality without the mythology. While some such groups do currently exist, we don't find a strong tradition of them with connections to Early Modern Wicca. In other words, while it may well be that Wicca has an air of permissiveness regarding such things, they aren't nearly as related as some people think. Those people with the opinion that Wicca is essentially a "fetishist excuse" have some basis for their hypotheses, but—at least in my opinion—lack enough evidence to make such statements conclusively.

Put simply, it is certainly *possible* that this idea of Wicca as a sexual liberator is one, genuine, psychological motivation for its founding. The only way to prove this conclusively false would probably be to have some sort of intensive record of psychotherapy sessions with Gardner and Wicca's other founders, showing that they had an opposition to such things. That record simply does not exist. Secondary sources such as the accounts of friends, some will argue, don't speak to subconscious drives. And for that matter, even psychotherapy might not have reached these drives if they were there but well-buried. However, it does not seem to be a very logical explanation for the existence of Wicca, especially considering that issues like dissatisfaction with non-sexual aspects of society are addressed loudly in Wicca's foundational documents—but sex is not.

If those who advocate this belief wish to convince me of it, I would need to see evidence for the existence of sexually-based spin-off groups from Early Modern Wicca, at least—groups that have the imagery and perhaps ritual structure of Wicca, but none of the religious aspects. Until that evidence appears, I view the sexual liberator hypothesis as interesting but unlikely. That being said, it makes me proud that my community can discuss it openly; I'm sure other communities would not accept such explicit discussion of the potential fallibility of their leaders and/or founders.

Modern Wicca solves the Lord and Lady problem with a new Theological Vector.

Modern Wicca (and Post-Modern Wicca) solves the issue of who the Lord and Lady are in a different way than Wicca did beforehand. Rather than focus on them as actual singular entities, either as a result of believing them the ancient deities of a pre-existing religion or by believing them to be deities revealed to a singular founder or core coven, this later Modern Wicca sees the deities as the actual results of the UPG of the individual. In other words, the neophyte is taught to seek and find the deity that speaks to him/her personally, and with whom s/he can have an actual relationship.

This is a major theological difference from the Original Core Theology (OCT) of Wicca. Many believe that any dramatic and widespread change from an OCT is either indicative of a flaw in that OCT or a flaw in the distribution of it beyond the core coven or founder. As an ethical eclectic looking at the OCT skeptically, I can see that both phenomena occur in the transmission of Wicca. The flaw in the OCT most prominent in Wicca's history occurred where early Wicca went one way and science another… and later Wicca took the path science had made, not their elders. The second example, the flaw in distribution, is primarily seen in the transmission of language and terms. "Samhain," "athamé" and "Hecate," for example, all have standardized pronunciations earlier in Wicca and today seem to be pronounced seemingly randomly—a fact no doubt stemming from the mispronunciations of elders or the inability of teaching resources like books to adequately transmit pronunciation.

The question of the source of the modern approach to gods in Wicca—that of patronage and UPG—is a valid one, if difficult to answer. In my opinion, at least, this change from the OCT is again a result both of poor transmission and of a flaw in the OCT itself, a flaw that was so broad and so intense that we don't see it maintained often, even in those groups whose practice is closest to the OCT today. Rather than reinterpret the old maiden-whore dichotomy Wicca more or less chose to write it off and pick up new theological approaches to the divine altogether: the triune goddess of maiden, mother and crone; patron and matron deities; gender kathenotheism[6] and the like.

These new vectors are so different from the original ideas that it can be argued that Modern Wicca is actually a completely different religion from Early Modern Wicca. My preference is, instead, for the realization that these new theological vectors are a result of the actions and practices of Early Modern Wicca: valid actions, rites and practices that led to the inevitable discovery of a refined approach to deity. Once these Early Modern Wiccan rites led to a discovery of a refined approach, there was no need to continue with the rougher and more difficult approach. We had discovered what it was that worked by looking for "whatever works."

As a caveat here, I will not say that I am unfamiliar with the idea held by some Modern Gardnerians (and others) that this newer Wicca, with these newer practices, isn't Wicca at all. What I will state, instead, is that reform movements in religion regularly result in sects that differ significantly from the original in important ways, and that while movements closer to the original religion tend to see these reform movements as illegitimate, there are philosophical reasons to distinguish reform movements from new movements. In other words, while there are, in fact, groups that use the term Wicca with no legitimate claim on the term, there are also groups with a strong theological claim to the term that are distinct from Gardner's Wicca. In fact, I would say that modern Gardnerians are also distinct from Gardner's Wicca and are, themselves, a reform movement.

---

[6] Kathenotheism where the male "all-god" is worshipped part of the year and the female "all-goddess" is worshipped the rest of the time.

Recommended Reading for Topic Thirteen:

Villa Of The Mysteries:
http://jcccnet.johnco.cc.ks.us/~jjackson/villa.html

Witchcraft Today. [Gerald Gardner]

The Witch-cult in Western Europe. [Margaret Murray]

Discussion Questions for Topic Thirteen:

13.1. What are some of the names of the god and goddess in Early Modern Wicca that have since been made accessible?

13.2. What do you notice the most about these names?

13.3. How did the gods with no names come to be?

13.4. How did the gods of many names come to be?

13.5. How is "Somn" different from the idea of a goddess who is all the deities of a pantheon?

13.6. What is the historic role of the sacred whore in mythology?

13.7. Identify some of the ways Modern Wicca approaches the problems of deity. Which do you expect to continue in Wicca's next fifty years?

Topic Fourteen: Wiccan Names

What is a Wiccan or Eke name? Why do we use them? What is the history of them? How do other people use them? Should I have one?
What on earth is an eke name?

Etymologically speaking, an "eke name" is the same as a nickname. "Eke" meant "also" or "extra," as those familiar with Chaucer might remember. The term "nickname" comes from the Middle English "eke name," and was created by a process known as "wrong division." In the case of "eke name," the term was eventually changed to nickname by a misunderstanding of the indefinite article "an" at a time when the language was chiefly verbal, not written. Over time "an eke name" came to be "a neke name," and thence to "a nickname."

Etymology not withstanding, though, in a Wiccan context "an eke name" refers to the name you go by as part of a circle, tradition or group. Also called a Witch name, Wiccan name or spirit name, for some, eke names are nothing more than a fancy sounding pseudonym used to make one sound more unique or scary. For most of us, however, eke names are genuine and heartfelt religious designations with deep meanings, often at both the spiritual and personal level. They represent not just what we are, but also our place in the greater community. With that in mind, is it surprising that so many early names had "of the Wica" attached to them? Our religion, like our family, had become a defining part of who we were.

While it is true that many solitary practitioners currently choose their craft name, historically craft names were used as part of identification within a community and were meaningless outside of that community. Indeed, unless only you and your gods know your craft name—a valid choice, I might add—you are using the name as part of a community, even if that community is difficult to define. Even if you call yourself "Stephanie Roundbottom Skytop," you are often making an implication about who you are and what you're doing. Often the epithet "of the Wica" or "of the community of Wiccans" or even "of such and such a tradition," is implied, even if not stated. A craft name (save for those secret names known only to the gods) is not about your identity in general, but about your identity in the community, specifically.

In my experience, these community craft names come in three varieties. While not a definitive list, eke names can be divided into Names of Choice, Names of Practice and Names of Initiation.

Names of Choice are names that a person invents or takes as a result of a desire to use a new name. These are similar to screen names and may reflect the personal likes of the user. A bobcat loving woman, who loves copper and sheep as well, might call herself "Lady Copper Bobcatsheep." As you may expect, these names can get very silly. In my experience, the Lady Copper Bobcatsheep of the world generally are called things like Sarah or Stephanie, and the Lady Bobcat nonsense is used only when writing indignant letters to the press or making websites.

These names are the lowest level of craft name, generally not of much value, often with little meaning and often very silly. It behooves you to think about your name clearly, and one method I use is to simply sleep on it for a few nights. If "Lady Copper Bobcatsheep" doesn't sound silly to you after rolling it around in your mouth a few times, you're welcome to it as a name of choice because, put simply, it is your choice. However, if you are concerned with being laughed at, it may be a name worth re-thinking.

Names of Practice, on the other hand, are names chosen to reflect a spiritual practice. This may be a dedication name, such as when you say "I am Steve, and from this day forward I shall be known as Dragonfire of the Wicca." These names are similar to the above names in that people usually pick them themselves. The difference, however, is seen in the fact these names usually are taken to represent a new practice in one's life, and are not merely a representation of one's likes or a desire to have a cool or scary-sounding name. A Name of Practice can be chosen when one discovers one's patron or matron deities, when one dedicates oneself to a new religion or tradition, when one marries or at another life-changing event. In many cultures, people assume a new name at adulthood, and this name of practice is similar to that name; it is a name of "Wiccanhood," if you will... a name used to describe the new you, who is not the same as the old, non-Wiccan you. This is an important distinction between a Name of Practice and a Name of Choice: A Name of Choice is taken merely from the desire to have a craft name, and does not mark a life turning point. A Name of Practice is taken for a reason beyond mere desire.

Both types of names have the potential to be silly, although one hopes that Names of Practice, because of the more serious nature of the reasons for taking such a name, will not be so... or will, at the least, be much less so.

Lastly, *Names of Initiation* are names given on the entry into a coven or tradition. They may be chosen, usually with guidance, or they may be given. An initiation is a formalized entry ritual into a group or tradition, and Names of Initiation are a group decision. Note that this differs from Names of Practice taken upon entry into a tradition or coven in that it is a formal occasion in which the naming is a part of the official initiatory ceremony. The name may be private, or you may have a private and public name. The choice of such a name is tradition-based and often oathbound. The naming ceremony and the way the names are assigned is similarly not my right to reveal, but an example of a similar practice from fiction might make it clear:

> Stilgar nodded, tugging at his beard. "I see strength in you... like the strength beneath a pillar." Again he paused, then: "You shall be known among us as Usul, the base of the pillar. This is your secret name, your troop name. We of Sietch Tabr may use it, but none other may so presume... Usul."-Frank Herbert, Dune

This example is excellent because most Wiccan groups that give names give two: a name, often long, that is used in contact with other Pagans, and a shorter name used within the immediate coven. This is similar to a nickname but better guarded. To reveal this name to the general public is generally forbidden, and is, at the very least, inappropriate. This would be similar, I suppose, to listing my *nom de plume* as "Mommy" or "Hun," which I am sure the Library of Congress would not appreciate in the slightest.

What were the purposes of craft names in Early Modern Wicca?

Many of the historical reasons for the use of craft names are based on the fact that Wicca is an initiatory mystery religion that, in its infancy, taught that it was a religion that was thousands of years old or that it was a new religion very heavily based on an ancient religion that had been pushed to the point of extinction. Thus the historical (by which I generally mean greater than 40 years old, since the history of Wicca is not much longer) use of the names is directly intertwined with those myths, sometimes inextricably. It is perhaps surprising, then, to see how common the idea of magical or craft names has become. Despite the fact that the traditional Ceremonial Magic method is to over-identify yourself to the universe ("I am Joe, son of Steve, who was the son of Fred who lived in the Lower East Side until 1970, and it is by the blood of my ancestors I command you!") this predominantly Wiccan phenomena has spread to many corners of the Pagan and Magical communities, often with a complete lack of understanding as to the reasons they were used to begin with.

When I say that Wicca was an initiatory mystery religion, of course I mean that early in Wicca, membership was limited only to those who had undergone an initiation rite, and advancement was limited to those who went through a mystery rite. In (or after) the mystery and initiation rites, a person agreed to abide by the rules of the group and received, in return, the divine knowledge reserved for group members. Included in this knowledge of the divine was the bestowing of a craft name, the secret name used within the group. Often the achievement of a secondary or tertiary rite led to a secondary or tertiary name. Many of these names, as discussed previously, were secret to the group, or even known only to the highest of elders, the gods and the one who bore them.

In Early Modern Wicca, this name served three basic purposes. The first of these purposes was that it maintained secrecy within the group. For example, in the traditional group to which I was first introduced, calling the leader by her first name within the group was considered bad form. We all knew her legal name. In fact, upon driving to her house we saw it predominantly displayed on her mailbox at the end of the driveway... but within the confines of the group, and when gathered for the purpose of conducting ritual, we called her by one of her craft names.

It is often claimed that this very secrecy is how Witchcraft survived the Witch-trials. Even under torture you cannot admit the names of those you do not know. There is really no proof at all this is true, but it is intuitively true, something that we know would be true if it actually had happened. It is much more difficult to trace, oh, Lady Copper Bobcateagle, than it is to trace, oh,

Kaatryn MacMorgan (especially since I'm all over the web, on amazon.com and listed with the copyright office of the Library of Congress, not to mention the IRS). These craft names likely exist because one of the elements of the OCT is that the Christian church has persecuted Wiccans in the past and is likely to do so in the future. While few still believe that, these names do offer, in addition to privacy, a sort of protection from the inquisition which, as we all know (she said sarcastically) is lurking around the corner waiting to pounce.

In addition to the protection and privacy of the craft names, it also adds a sense of equality within the group. Bill Gates and Donald Trump could be in my coven, but they would still be Lords Moonbottom and Fluffyback, regardless of their status as premier capitalists. Their last names or their outside identities would mean nothing. If you consider that Wicca is, at its heart, a singularly British tradition, this becomes even more obvious. Family names, history and more mean nothing. Spencer, Windsor, Morgan, Campbell, Douglas or Smith, you're all on par in the circle.

As I've hinted at, these names also represent that the person with the name has experienced a mystery. A mystery is a rite sacred to a god, pantheon or tradition in particular and undergoing that mystery or even witnessing it (depending on the rite) changes your status with the divine. This status change may be the revelation of new material, such as the names or the gods, or it may even be granting you the keys to an afterlife of choice. Mysteries are not a Wiccan thing, and I speak here in the most general terms of mysteries. An example of a mystery accessible to the Western culture, albeit not a particularly dramatic or complex one, is the Christian rite of baptism. During baptism, a child takes or is given a new name, and often adults who are baptized do the same. This occurs again if a person becomes a priest or monk, and it is not different in Wicca, with many changing their names to reflect the mystery rite.

Early Modern Wicca, therefore, had three true established reasons for these craft names long before they become a New Age fashion statement. These names assured privacy and protection from a perceived force out to destroy Wicca, made the coveners equal regardless of family name or history and indicated that a person had participated in a mystery rite. To all but the most cynical, who can write the use of craft names by solitaries off as nothing less than me-too-ism, it becomes clear that as Wicca moved from a predominantly initiatory religion of small groups to a religion that involved many solitary practitioners, the reasons for taking craft names changed as well, or else we'd see their usage dwindling.

Why do solitaries and other practitioners of Modern Wicca use craft names?

Most covens still use craft names for many of the same reasons they did during Early Modern Wicca. Even in those groups that do not believe, for example, that the inquisition is out to get them, the adoption of new names as if they were lurking around every corner is often a good tie to the practices of their spiritual ancestors who did believe in such a manner. Coveners, in short, use craft names for the same reasons their ancestors did, even if they don't believe in the same things that lead to the creation of the craft-name concept. Therefore, the discussion of the use of craft names in Modern Wicca beyond the identical uses previously discussed is very much the discussion of the use of such names by solitary practitioners.

For many solitaries, this new name is little more than what we previously called "names of choice," a name taken with the intention of little more than changing your name. These are similar to screen names. Few of us netheads remain joe01823634@usol.com for our entire time on the net. We become, instead, JoeLadyLvr or GODwasCoPilot-WeCrshdInMtsNI8Hm, names that reflect something of our personality, but not things we'd generally introduce ourselves with[7]. Many solitaries take names that they are willing to use in emails or in letters to the press or on official sounding documents but still use nicknames or their birth names in all personal affairs.

I am sure there is a deep meaning behind such pseudonyms, but I am unsure such usage is a spiritual one. A solitary may, of

[7] I did once tell a guy who was stumbling over my name at a New Year's party that my friends just call me "Kat@cuew.org," but I think the copious amount of champagne I'd consumed had more to do with that than identifying myself by email address.

course, create a name similar to a name of initiation upon performing a rite of dedication, but I do not see such rites are identical to initiations and do not, personally, understand the need to consider them the same as initiations, which are, of course, all about membership in a group. This is tangential to the discussion at hand, however, so I'll let it drop.

Solitaries may choose a secret name used when working with and talking to the gods, a name for documents and the like because they feel a need for secrecy or a name they chose specifically to interact with the greater Wiccan community, but the main point is that a solitary doesn't have to choose a name unless they are practicing within a tradition. If they are practicing within a tradition, they have that tradition's guidelines to use, and if they are atraditionals they may use whatever method they wish or simply choose to not have any name at all.

The "why" is mostly about a matter of choice. A nontraditional solitary may or may not use a craft name as they see fit. They may choose it as a name of practice, a name that reflects their status as "one of the Wica" or as a name of choice — one of those "just because" names that many have. We can hope no one chooses them for no reason at all, but no doubt there are a few out there who have them merely because other people have them and they have become convinced, for whatever reason, that they are obligated to have one as well.

The Use of Names and Naming in Magic

Another important aspect of the use of names is in magical practice. Some traditions and covens keep eke names secret in order to protect their members; traditionalists who believe the Wiccan religion is an ancient one believe this derives chiefly from their practice, as they, and their members had to protect one another's identities from prosecution during "olden times." In some senses, this would be made easier by referring to each other with craft or eke names. Gardner's "Old Laws" were (and are) quite explicit as to the importance of keeping this information safe from the ears of persecuting officials.

Most Pagan traditions, whether they see an ancient history in Wicca or not, still hold that each individual Wiccan, Druid, Asatruar or other Pagan should have the choice as to whether to reveal his or her religion… staying in or coming out of the broom closet, as it were. In a very real way, the knowledge of someone's true name was also a way to have power over that person.

This isn't a new idea, by any means. In the Jewish tradition, the name of God was too holy to be spoken or even written with all its proper vowels. It was generally written with four consonants: yod, heh, vah and heh, which some Christians render as Yahweh (and some shuffle and mispronounce as Jehovah). Some people know these four consonants as the Tetragrammaton. It's not important to get into the Tetragrammaton or Qabbalah in depth here. Suffice it to say that magically and religiously speaking, names are believed to have power. As another example, much of the "study" of demonology centered around learning a demon's true name in order to gain power over it.

Even in the scientific linguistic arena, however, there are areas of study respecting the possible relationship between the spoken word and the object referred to, called phonosemantics. Please note that this is the study of the *possible* relationship; most linguists take the opposing position and contend that there is no intrinsic "sound symbolism."

Nonetheless, there is a long tradition of such study, scientifically-based or not, and it is from this tradition that Wicca derives its use of craft or eke names.

How some traditions choose names

As I have indicated, the choice of names varies from group to group. In general they follow two patterns, names drawn from lists and names formed by a special technique. List names are easy to describe, they include virtue-names, similar to the Christian virtue names we are familiar with from the Puritans: Mercy, Grace, Hope, and Chastity. Wiccans my use different virtues, however: Happiness, Joy, and Wisdom, for example. These also include names taken from nature, with each name having a particular relevance: Autumn, Tree, Buck, Star, Sky and Melody. For groups that use those names, there may be only a handful allowed, or they may be whatever name the person finds apt.

More stringent list names may follow different patterns. For example, some groups, for reasons that I will not comment upon, have their members draw their names from lists of those executed for alleged acts of Witchcraft or heresy. Still others have a small list of characteristics that match each name and give that name to members of their group with the appropriate characteristics. I have personally been attached to such a group. I have also witnessed groups where joining requires a change in last name or where being a member means that you will have a name similar to the name of your teacher or leader. Names may be chosen from lists of colors, gemstones or animals. Names may also be chosen from the names of the gods, but this practice brings up a completely new set of problems.

More common, though perhaps less interesting, are those groups for whom the creation of a name follows a pattern. This may be a combination of lists where you take one from column A and one from column B, or it may be done through the use of numerology, scrying or even picking scrabble letters out of a bag. Each of these techniques has benefits and flaws. Random names are often difficult to pronounce. Names that take from two columns and slam them together often sound silly, and names that use numerology open up questions about the legitimacy of numerology.

I am, personally, a fan of virtue names. If I had joined a trad where such a name was created I often wonder what my virtue would be. Introspection? Sarcasm? Laughter? Critical? How's that for a Craft name: Critical MacMorgan? We could name my son Crisis and my wife Urgent — we'd be Urgent, Crisis and Critical MacMorgan... No, I don't think so.

There are, however, lovely virtue names out there — Wisdom, Liberty, Freedom — but our culture tells us such names are feminine. In part, this is because the Christians whose virtue names we are most familiar with gave biblical names to the men and virtue names to the women (possibly because the Bible lacks more than a handful of names for women). Perhaps we can consider that in the future, and name ourselves after our founders. We can call ourselves names like Gerald, Doreen, Raymond and Colin, good stout Western European names. Gosh, I hope not. What's the point in having a secret name known only to your clan, tribe or coven that is the same as your neighbor's legal name?

Of course, that opens up another set of questions altogether about what a name is and why we should reject one. List names, we know, are easy. Naming programs that give everyone born on January 1st one name and those born on January 2nd another also have their benefits. Numerology and randomness make silly combinations of letters and naming yourself after dead Christians killed by other dead Christians opens up a whole can of worms of impropriety. Naming yourself after gods is hubris... or after saints or people who inspired you is often seen as posturing. Is it any wonder, then, that more of us go by a small set of socially acceptable names than try something new?

The best way to choose a name

I am often asked by people who do not have a tradition with a naming convention what I feel is the best way to choose a name. The best way in such cases, no holds barred, is whatever way allows you to have a name that you are comfortable with and has no negative side effects. For example, previously we mentioned groups that used the names of people killed for Witchcraft as their craft names. If you believe that the dead are aware of the living's thoughts towards them this is a strong double-edged sword. On the one hand, these names assure that the people killed, who were killed unjustly, are remembered as having been killed unjustly. On the other, these people, most of whom were Christians, many of whom belonged to radical sects and were only slightly less aggressive in their Christianity than those who killed them, are having what they would consider evil witchcraft — the worship of other gods — done in their name.

Imagine that you were killed for being female, even though you were male and had no hint of femininity whatsoever. You were killed merely because your neighbor convinced people you were female despite all the evidence to the contrary. Would you, if you were capable of being aware of what was going on after death, want people naming their daughters after you? How about holding you up as an example of feminine virtue? You probably wouldn't like it. In fact, you'd probably find it disrespectful!

This is the problem with using the names of those killed as witches as craft names: they weren't witches. In fact, they probably went kicking and screaming to their graves insisting they weren't and praying wholeheartedly that someone, anyone, would believe them. To those who believe in ghosts and the like, many of these people are probably highly unhappy spirits, and adding them to your life is a bad idea. To those who don't believe in such things, but generally think the dead are best left alone, it's still a bad idea.

Worse yet, as far as unintended effects, is naming yourself after a deity. Some deity names have become so common in our lexicon that it's hard to imagine the deities are offended by it, but to call yourself by a god's name when you believe in that god is, at best, disrespectful of that deity's name. The closest I can come to a suitable metaphor here is that of having a best friend and suddenly deciding that you and your best friend have the same name. It is confusing, at the least, and probably disrespectful.

For some deities, it is even worse because calling yourself by their names is claiming a relationship with them that you don't have. For those of us who believe the gods punish excessive pride the fine line here is obvious and not something to be crossed when avoidable. Thus naming yourself after a god is a bit more risk than we are willing to take.

As with all things, the choice of a name is something that, approached carefully, can have wide latitude. A few extra minutes of research alone can spare you uncomfortable moments. In addition, by thinking long and hard about a name, you know that it is more than just something you picked out of thin air. When you test it, research it and pray about it your name becomes something more — a part of you.

The Nitty Gritty

Whether you are choosing a *Name of Choice* or *Name of Practice* for yourself, or if you are helping to choose a *Name of Initiation* for someone else in your coven or tradition, it should be a thoughtful, spiritual process. Forcing a choice usually results in a name that may be lovely, but somehow does not precisely fit. Such a name may always seem to be missing something fundamental. If it is your name of choice, you may find yourself changing names every year or perhaps even every month in an attempt to hit on a name that would be truly appropriate, appropriate in a way that your impulsive forced choices never will be.

Things to keep in mind while choosing an eke name:

1. Accept that finding the right name may be a long process. It is better to go without an eke name while the choice is being made than to choose something that is not right for you, and answer to an eke name that is not appropriate. If your eke name is meant to be a secret

name, shared only with the gods, be assured that they will know who you are even if you don't know, yet, what your eke name should be. If your eke name is meant to be shared with a community, you are doing a disservice to other members of that community by causing them to address you with a name you mean only to be a temporary stopgap, and causing them to know you by a name that doesn't fit who you truly are.

2. Similarly, an eke name should not be an expression of only one aspect of your personality, unless perhaps you mean it to represent the spiritual side of yourself. This is the problem with many *Names of Choice:* that fixing on one or more of your favorite things and adopting them as a name can mean that the name will cease to be appropriate should your favorites change as you learn and grow in the future. If you regard your name choice as something that should represent deep, permanent aspects of yourself, you will be better served.

3. You should never choose a name based on what you think its effect will be on other people. However, understanding how your name will be regarded by your community is a good idea. There is a difference between choosing a name for effect in your community, and choosing one that will communicate something about you to your community. If I were to choose a name like "Lady Darkmoon" because I thought it would give the impression of someone elegant and slightly goth, it might not be the best choice. On the other hand, if I chose "Lady Darkmoon" because my matron goddess is especially connected to the dark phase of the moon, and because I felt the deepest connection to her at the new moon, it might be an appropriate choice indeed.

4. Feel free to explore various techniques for choosing names. Buckland recommends using numerology to choose a craft name, and some people feel strongly that numerology is necessary to the process. Other people find such a system cumbersome, and believe it is more helpful to choose names that can connect them to a particular pantheon — for example, a Celtic name to help them feel connected to an Irish pantheon. What is most

important when exploring these techniques is that your choice is consistent with your personal practice. In other words, if you never use numerology in your personal practice, it might not be helpful to incorporate it into the process of choosing your craft name. On the other hand, if you use numerology frequently in your practice, your name may never feel "right" if you don't use numerology to make sure your name is appropriate for you.

5.   Once you have found your name — or one has been found for you — make absolutely sure you understand what the context of its use should be. If it is meant to be a name used anytime you are wearing the mantle of Wiccan, or Wiccan Priest/ess, use it appropriately. If it is meant to be a name that is shared only within the larger community of Wiccans and Pagans, use it within that community. If it is meant to be a secret name, to be revealed only to the members of your tradition, your coven or your inner circle, use it only there. And be aware of how others choose to use their eke names, as well. If you are privy to the secret name of someone else, a name that should not be revealed in certain contexts, be aware of that. Even if it is not an oathbound issue, but merely an issue of respect for the wishes of another individual , you should not reveal a name that is meant to be secret without a damn good reason.

Discussion Questions for Topic Fourteen:

14.1. What are the distinctions between names of initiation, choice and practice?

14.2. What are some of the many other names for "craft names," what do they mean?

14.3. Ceremonial Magicians rarely use such pseudonyms because they feel that identifying themselves to The All should be as specific as possible. What does this say about the Wiccans practice, if anything?

14.4. What are some ways that names are chosen in traditions?

14.5. Why do solitaries generally not need craft names?

Topic Fifteen: We Meet on the Moons?

What is the importance of the moon in Wicca? What is meant when people talk about the addition of the moon cult to Wicca? What are the "moons" and should we just chuck the concept altogether?

Read Error

A commonly believed concept in Wicca is that there are 26 lesser holidays in the Wiccan year, called Esbats, which take place on the full and new moons. While it is true that most Wiccans do celebrate the full and/or the dark of the moon, this is a later addition to the religion itself. In fact, most Early Modern Wiccan groups taught that the best time to meet was on the full moon; a smaller chunk of EMWs taught it was better to meet on the new moon, or both... but not because the moon itself was sacred.

Esbats, in fact, were not originally designed to be worship dates, so it would be odd to place them on sacred nights. In their original structures, both in Early Modern Wicca and in pre-Wiccan tales of Witchcraft, esbats are business meetings — small get-togethers, often just of leadership, in which the next Sabbat was planned, students were taught and other plans were laid. It is not unusual for an esbat to not involve a ritual at all, so to teach that they require rituals, especially moon rituals, is erroneous.

The idea of meeting on either the full or the dark of the moon is rooted in Murray's *The Witch-cult in Western Europe*, which was so instrumental in the creation of Modern Wicca. This imagined Witch-cult met on the full moon more out of convenience than out of sacred belief. Groups of these imagined Witches convened on the full moon because it was during the full moon that it was easiest to travel. Conversely, groups of other Witches met on the dark of the moon so that they would not be seen. No stories exist of groups meeting on both, which makes sense. Those meeting on the full moons for ease of travel would, by definition, not travel on the new moon, and those using the darkness of the new moon as cover would see no point in meeting by the full moon.

The imagined Witches of these Esbats, dragging brooms be-hind them[8] to cover their trails and meeting on secret hilltops and forest glades monthly, or whenever they could, are allegedly the source of the modern so-called stereotype of a Witch... the one with the pointed hat and broom, cavorting in the wild with imps and worse. Despite being an imagined phenomenon, they are also the idea behind the initial meeting style of Modern Wic-cans. We do not meet on the full moon because we hold the moon sacred. Indeed, holding the moon sacred in the way many people do today is an utterly modern concept. Instead, we meet on the moons because these alleged spiritual ancestors did, and they did so more out of convenience than anything else.

So where does the idea that all Wiccans hold the moon sa-cred come from? In part, it is another example of a reading error in the new Wicca. These reading errors are, in and of themselves, not bad things, because they allow us to examine our faith more in-depth. They would be less common if we had more physical teachers and less reliance on books, but that is not really indica-tive of the superiority of real world teachers so much as it is in-dicative that the best education is a balanced one. We don't have such errors when we interact with a large group — it's just that simple.

In my opinion, such reading errors come from simple ques-tions that are not answered by teachers and books because peo-ple assume you know what they mean. When I hear *"Whenever you have need of me, and better it should be in the full of the moon,"* I can assume that what other people hear is what I do — that the goddess of The Charge is telling me to meet with my brethren whenever I have need of her and that it is best to do so on the full of the moon. I do not hear that the moon is sacred, and in-deed, less than half of the goddesses named in The Charge can be said to be lunar goddesses. The entire Wiccan Liturgical cal-endar is solar, so why would I think for a moment that she

---

[8] I am aware that some claim the "right way" to ride a broom is like a hobby-horse, with the brush in front. However, this "dragging the broom behind them" is supposedly one of the sources for the popular images of the Witch on her broom, and I think claiming there is a right way is absolutely silly. Of course, given the choice, I ride in airplanes, and prefer vacuum cleaners to brooms, so what would I know?

meant anything other than the words before me? Indeed, coupled with the knowledge that few of the Early Modern Wiccans met on every full moon, I find myself unable to hear anything but the words before me.

It is not surprising then, that many Modern Wiccans use the full and new moons as gather-as-you-may dates — either to establish coven meetings or classes, to do emergency rituals to pray for an ill member or just as a convenient time to meet new members. This is more in line with the original idea of an esbat as business time than as true moon worship.

That's not to say moon worship is forbidden, or not Wiccan, just that it's not a requirement of Wiccan worship. In other words it is something to add if your UPG agrees with it, and something to remove if it does not. This sort of thinking — recognizing where things come from and removing them if you have good reason to — is what I feel separates the dabbling nonsense of do-whatever-you-like from the careful modification of practice to make it relevant both to the individual and to the historical Wiccan community.

What did Early Modern Wiccans think ancient "witches" did on the full moon and why?

Murray's Satan worshipping Witch-Cult (who, of course, followed a Satan that wasn't *really* the Satan of Christianity) met on great Sabbats determined by a solar calendar, as well as at lesser meetings, the business-like Esbats. Murray doesn't place these holy days on the full moons, and it isn't surprising that Early Modern Wiccans also don't generally place them on specific dates, preferring to meet instead on dates of astrological importance or in times of need.

In fact, Early Modern Wiccans *didn't* generally meet on the full moons at all, save when it was a good means to an end. The addition of the full moons to the liturgical calendar of Wicca comes late in the game, as the idea of the women's spirituality, through the Dianic Pagan movement, enters Wicca. The full moon in the earliest of Early Modern Wicca was not something that dictated meetings, but instead it provided a union of Indo-European mythologies into the practice.

There were three distinct benefits to adding moon ritual, imagery and mythology to Wicca. Early Modern Wicca taught that the religion of the Witch-Trials, detailed in Murray's *Witch-Cult*, was the religion that this new Witchcraft was either based upon or a surviving sect of. The amount of literalism applied to this myth varied from group to group, ranging from the most literal, who taught that their witchcraft was literally handed down in secret from a spiritual ancestor from before the coming of Christianity… to the least literal, who saw their new religion as, at the most, a reconstruction of a likely pre-Christian indigenous belief that was lost, but whose artifacts allowed a sort of reverse-engineering of beliefs. By adding the moon to the liturgy, Early Modern Wiccans reinforced the idea of Wicca being primitive, added a category of liturgy it had not had in the past and allowed a body of mythology to be added to the mythology within Wicca.

Chief amongst the problems of this addition, and the one perhaps quoted the most, was that before the lunar imagery was added, beyond a few ritual names, the cult worship of Freya had already taken hold in Early Modern Wicca. For many groups, Freya, or Freya-like deities, were the images of the goddess of the primal myth of Wicca — the descent of the goddess. Freya had by this time been associated with the moon by a small fragment of authors of comparative mythology, but in her core pantheon she was a solar goddess, as was Persephone, to a lesser extent. These goddesses (who perhaps can be called "winter goddesses" but otherwise bear little similarity to each other) are associated with the reduction of sunlight in winter, with descent into the underworld, with life and death but not, despite attempts to link them in that manner, with the moon.

The Witches of Murray's Witch-cult were likewise unaffiliated with the moon; according to the witch-trial records, their rites were held on full moons sporadically, but not as a part of their alleged religion. In other words, like other certain signs of witchcraft, full moon practice alone was not used as a claim of "witchcraft," but as evidence thereof. Taking this into consideration, however, if you assume, as Gardner seems to, that the witches of Murray's Witch-cult and the faeries of British mythology are one and the same — or even that they merely have some relationship, as Murray tries to indicate — then you can see the bleeding of one mythology into another.

While Witches don't gather under the full of the moon any more than on other days (and considerably less than on certain

Christian feast days), according to legends, faeries do. By uniting the Witch myth with the faerie myth, you allow the ideas of the faerie-folk, such as faerie rings, mischief, dancing in the moonlight and messing with poor farmers, to become the myths of the Witches. That indigenous Europeans generally considered neither faeries nor witches benign was unimportant, because before Witchcraft came on the scene faeries had already been recast as sweet and helpful in the public eye. One must wonder, however, if an intention to recast Witches in the public eye was the motive behind the connection. After all, if faeries could be recast, surely Witches could as well.

It becomes a very reasonable question to ask if the goal of Wicca is this very recasting of Witches in a new light. While some no doubt try to do this, or feel it is their job, I think most Wiccans feel that the job of Wicca, if it can be said to be a job, is to provide for worship of the gods. However, the recasting of Witches in a new light was most assuredly something Murray was invested in, and it does translate into Wicca, as much of her work does, as a result of Wicca's founders' investment in Murray's writings. In other words, while Wicca was not directly invested in recasting Witches in a new (and inaccurate) light, Murray was, and since Early Modern Wicca was invested in upholding Murray's works, it was sucked into her personal aspirations.

The addition of the cult of the moon to Modern Wicca

Doing a websearch for "lunar cults" gives you lots of information on science fiction games, new Wiccan and Wiccanesque rites and bizarre fringe Christian beliefs about alleged Satanic practice... but very little about any ancient peoples. While it is true many ancient cultures revered the moon in one form or another, and true that many ancient religions worshipped on the full moon (amongst other times), the linking of the moon with magical life is a fairly modern invention. Only perhaps with the Maya, who the Eurocentric anthropologists of Gardner's day ignored, do we see a true cult of the moon slightly reminiscent of the one that gets added to Wicca.

The addition of this body of myth, liturgy and teaching that I call the cult of the moon to Wicca is an attempt to take a religion that claimed to be primitive and add *astrolatry*, the worship of astronomical bodies, to it. Such an addition provided a number of benefits to the fledgling religion. By aligning with astrolatry, which Christianity loathed, it further affirmed its distinctness from Christianity. By taking an element of what they termed "primitive" faith they reaffirmed that theirs was an ancient religion and connected it, in one fell swoop, both to Mithraicism and HP Blavastsky's *The Secret Doctrine*, which often perches on the edge of becoming an apologia for astrolatry.

Astrolatry is not the worship of moon goddesses, but worship of the moon itself. Sometimes it is interpreted as the worship is of a deity that is seen as being symbolized by the moon, but most often, and most literally, astrolatry is the worship of the moon as a deity. This can be a hard distinction to understand, but essentially if you can grasp the idea that to true proponents of astrolatry those who landed on the moon were setting foot on a deity you can grasp the distinction between astrology and those for whom the moon is a symbol of their deity.

With that in mind, at times the earliest of Early Modern Wicca reads like an interview with a used car salesman. Perhaps you are familiar with the metaphor of the salesman with the perfect car for you. You begin with a car worth nothing, and as you ask the salesman about things he is legally obligated to do to sell the car he claims to have thrown those in already, even though he hadn't planned on doing them at all:

You: "Is the car ready to go?"

CS: "Of course, there are some paper work details, but those should only take a few minutes...."

You: "Has it been inspected?"

CS: "Of course!" (Makes note to inspect car.)

You: "And the title, you've done a search to make sure it wasn't a rebuild, right?"

CS: "We do that with all our cars! I'll look again, just to be sure. (Makes note to do a search before turning it over.)

And so it continues. Wicca, in its infancy, works pretty much the same way, with Gardner and his immediate spiritual descendants playing the part of the car salesman. "Is it an ancient religion?" "Why yes, of course!" "Does it have mysteries like an ancient religion?" "Why, yes — see these mysteries...?" "Does it have rites of passage like an ancient religion?" "Why, yes, we've just kept them secret until now!" "How about astrolatry?" "Yup! That, too!"

The only problem, similar to the used car I once watched a friend buy with the engine of a Honda, body of a Chevy and seats from a Volkswagen, is that we can tell that this Wicca is a Frankenfaith. None of the parts, early on, fit together particularly well. It works, but like having Freya as a lunar deity, it shows the seams and welds that hold it together, and each of those seams is a fault point. Ancient peoples worshipped the moon, or at least honored it, for completely different reasons, reasons that often gel poorly with Wicca.

One can also suppose that aligning a new faith with solar and lunar dates, based heavily on connections with nature and the natural world, was also another way to distinguish it from Abrahamic religions, which worshipped regularly every seventh day... a day seemingly unconnected to anything outside their own faith. For those who worship outdoors (by preference, at least) with none of the architecture of great cathedrals, temples or mosques to surround them, relying on the dome of the sky itself is ideal for an appropriate setting. After all, the solar and lunar calendars are global, and no matter your faith, you can observe the full or dark of the moon, and the height of the sun in the sky.

In a way, this is great PR work for Wicca and Paganism, but one can hardly think of it as a grand conspiracy, unless it is a conspiracy of poets. It's more a confabulation, a confusion of history in which fantasy is quite honestly mistaken for reality... in this context, one could regard it as having emerged from the ether, unconsciously. It seeks purchase; it seems plausible; it is accepted as factual. However it is NOT a factual account. It merely has the appearance of one.

Ronald Hutton's chapter on "Finding a Goddess" in *Triumph of the Moon* is enlightening for anyone interested in how a moon goddess came to be so associated with Modern Pagan Witchcraft and Wicca. Hutton suggests that the works of the Romantic poets like Keats and Shelley were pivotal in associating nature-worshippers, druids and pagans in the popular English imagination with "green" goddesses of beauty, the flowering earth and the moon.

Keep it or chuck it?

The moon is awe-inspiring. She inspires poetry and worship, songs, dances and temples. It figures in our literature, from the werewolf to the witch, and is said to be the seat of inspiration and also of lunacy — the very word a derivative of the name, Luna, the glowing moon. She controls the tides, and lights the night, and seems to swell and grow like a pregnant woman. She is a pure and noble sight in a world that we often see as corrupt and filthy.

As a practitioner of a spiritual regimen that has involved training my brain to snap me into reverie with the divine by visual and emotional cues, I see the moon and instantly pray. I have to think to do otherwise. That the moon has a vital place in my personal practice is an undeniable fact of my existence. I can remember, when I was younger, hypnotizing myself by looking at the moon through my window or reflected off water.

Yet my primary deity is generally, if inaccurately, portrayed as a solar deity. In addition, I am not the most new-agey, dancing-beneath-the-moon kind of person. I'm a pretty laid back, mellow person. For me, spirituality comes in two basic types: the strict regimen I've trained my brain to keep me in — prayers upon waking up, daily rituals and meditations and the like — and a more laid back, spontaneous practice. For me, prayers and rituals involving the moon always fall under the latter.

The question for me has never been whether or not the moon festivals should be celebrated, but if — by regulating them to a monthly occurrence, scheduled at a certain time and certain place — we are taking away from the wonder of the primitive astrolatry. I suspect part of this is prejudice regarding how and where I learned Wicca. In the clime I grew up in, between two mountain ranges, and between the Great Lakes and the Atlantic Ocean, the full moon was not always the easiest thing to see. I can remember, for that reason, particularly spectacular full moons, nights when the clouds across the sky hung around her like lace, or when she burned red in the humidity of an August night, the taste of salt potatoes and cinnamon taffy on my lips at the top of the Ferris Wheel at the State Fair, watching her rise over Sandy Beach while I felt my life beginning to change around me. These were intensely spiritual moments, not forced or planned for, but instead dictated by the universe itself.

I know from experience that trying to train myself to meet with my fellows on the full moon results in a feeling not altogether unlike wearing clothes that don't fit me or pretending to be something I'm not. However, when meetings coincide with the full moon, or when my people and I come together for some cause on the full moon, it is intensely spiritual. It is because of this experience that I can say, without any discomfort, that I find the idea of meeting on the full moon simply because it is full as artificial as meeting on Sunday because someone declares it the right day to meet. In other words, I feel we should not toss out the idea of meeting on the full moon, but instead the idea that we should meet merely because it is full. It is a subtle distinction, but an important one.

Toward a better understanding of lunar festivals

In a lunar calendar there are thirteen full moons in a (solar) year. None of these moons are "blue moons" because the blue moon (a term for a second full moon in a month) is, by definition, impossible in a lunar calendar. If we use a solar calendar instead, a calendar in which the rest of the Wiccan holidays fall quite nicely, we can incorporate the lunar festivals as sacred days by choice, days in which to celebrate our gods with our friends by choice and habit instead of by mandate, and these rare "blue moons" become a time for particular festivities.

The blue moon is not sacred because it occurs unexpectedly; it occurs right when it is supposed to! It is sacred because of its rarity. Contrary to the teachings of a few, we do not celebrate it because we look up in the sky and suddenly discover a second full moon in a single month and wonder at how that can be. As we all know, the blue moon is a perfectly logical thing, a result of having a calendar with months that are an average of 30 days long and a moon cycle that is slightly less than that. Using rarity, synchronicity and coincidence to honor the divine is an ancient practice, peoples throughout the world give special honor to times and places where things meet or that happen rarely. We worship and honor places that mark boundaries, from the shore to the edge of a cliff, and we honor those things that seem out of place-sacred boulders dropped in the middle of flat lands by glaciers, islands in the middle of steams, mountains, craters and pillars of rock that stick out of the flatlands, mesas in the mountains, rocky crags in the middle of worn old mountains, gentle slopes in the rocky crags of newer mountains. We rarely worship or hold as sacred the thing that is around us. I remember bringing a friend from the plains to Upstate New York, with its constant rolling hills and seeing her wonder at every twist and turn of I-81, things that were as natural to me as breathing or the sky being blue on a clear day (and as inspirational as breathing or blue skies, but that's a tangent)… and to her were these things of great wonder. We would crest a great hill, only to have another before us, and every time she would just be amazed because that's not what hills did in her brain.

This is an example of why the blue moon and other lunar festivals are important; they represent a change in status from the ordinary. The moon is not full nearly as often as it is less than full, so the full moon is more sacred than the rest of the phases. It is full twice in a month even less often than that, so we see the sacredness multiplied.

It is interesting, perhaps, that we tend to think that all cultures see these things the same way. In fact, while celebrations of the moon are common, many cultures ascribe to the moon holidays on the days that our own culture tends to see just as not full or new. The Horned Moon, about 3 days from the new, is the one that comes to mind right away, because I was raised hearing it called the Cheshire moon, since it resembles the grin left in the air after the Cheshire cat vanishes.

By changing the reason for meeting on the full moon from a dogmatic expression ("We meet on the full moons because they are full") to an expression of personal worship, we allow the full moons to begin to take on new characteristics. We can even, as some have done, compose calendars, creating a new festival for each full moon by associating the full moon in any month with a specific attribute. We can't do this without putting it in another calendar. If you create a thirteen month lunar calendar and declare that the 9th month is the harvest moon, it ceases to fall anywhere near the harvest within a few years — even faster if you make the calendar 12 months long. This is a strong indicator of the flaw in the many inauthentic "Celtic" or "ancient" lunar calendars found on the net that list the moons in the order they appear in the year. First, as has been demonstrated, if they have a blue moon, as most do, they can't be lunar at all, and secondly, if they list the 9th moon as a "harvest moon" or use similar seasonal attributes they are impossible to follow because the seasons are based on the movement of the sun, not the moon!

It is funny these calendars are so very often associated with the same ancient peoples who allegedly knew astronomy inside and out!

The confusion stems from the fact that many cultures did, indeed, call a month by an attribute or object. Our naming of modern cycles after Emperors and numbers is neither particularly ancient nor common. Let's return to the imaginary for a moment. The Logosians (the imaginary people mentioned in *Wicca 333*) have a calendar. This calendar names the 12 months as Oak, Holly, Ash, Jellyfish, Tuna, Pearl, Kitty-cat, and a bunch of other names. Like many ancient people, the reasons for these names are confusing, but it comes, in this case, from the way the Logosians see the universe as having been created. Long before people came to be, the gods created all the things that exist, say their legends, in a certain order. The months are called after the first twelve things the gods made, according to their faith.

As typically happens, when new Wiccans see this calendar and decide they like it, a few of them write of the new ancient Wiccan calendar and, not fully understanding the Logosian mythos, begin to attribute new things to the calendar. By the time it reaches the public eye, the idea that the months are named after the first twelve things the gods made is gone and it means something else altogether. In the past fifteen or so years I've watched this happen with the "Celtic" calendar amongst others, so again, I wish it was complete fiction, but it's not.

Regardless of the lack of historical legitimacy in saying, oh, the moon in August is the Harvest Moon, when you remove the idea that one must meet on the full moon because the moon is full, you can replace it with a better holiday. For example, August is the Sweet Corn harvest in my area, and our personal August holiday, which usually falls on the Saturday closest to the full moon, involves a celebration of the harvest. We will have, at the least, my famous journey-cake, studded with multicolored sweet corn and fresh butter, as part of our festival. More likely, we will have a huge party in which the fruits of the season are prominently featured. We will have this festival not because the moon is full but because it is the time of the harvest. Lunar festivals become, then, not festivals of the moon but festivals of the land around you which occur on the full moon because they needed to occur at some point in the month, and nights of the full moon were as good an evening as any.

Other groups have decided to forego lunar festivals entirely and meet, say, on the third Sunday of every month, just finding the attempt to unify the solar nature of agricultural festivals and the modern calendar with the lunar one too difficult and time consuming to bother with. This, too, is a valid approach to the problem, as is the approach taken by another friend, of having some of his group, which meets nearly ten times a month, plan events around the full moon while others plan events on a more conventional calendar, allowing people in his group to pick and choose from several free-form festivals in addition to his group's weekly ones each Sunday.

Recommended Reading for Topic Fifteen:

http://www.hermetic.ch/cal_stud/lunarcal/otherlun.htm
(A collection of Lunar calendars.)

Discussion Questions for Topic Fifteen:

15.1. What are some ancient lunar customs and traditions?

15.2. What is the difference between "and better it should be on the full moon" and "we meet because the moon is full"?

15.3. What did Early Modern Wiccans think witches did on the full moons and why?

15.4. Give a few examples of lunar imagery in Modern Wicca.

15.5. It has been said that the addition of lunar imagery coincides with the addition of Maiden-Mother-Crone ideas of deity, not surprisingly. What other things might be expected to have bled into Wicca at the same time?

Topic Sixteen: Sacred Space

What is Sacred Space? What is meant by the two distinct kinds? What are some of the Sacred Space concepts we may see in the Wicca of the future?

Concepts of sacred space in Wicca

There are several concepts of sacred space in Wicca, ranging from the smallest personal space — the temple of the body — to the largest — the idea of the planetary biosphere, or even the universe itself, as sacred. In between these two concepts lie the majority of our sacred spaces. For simplicity's sake, I discuss these spaces in terms of four basic concepts, as well as a fifth larger concept. The four basic ones will be discussed later, but for now I will attempt to discuss this larger concept: The idea that All-That-Is is sacred.

In *All One Wicca*, I discuss the fact that the term "sacred" has both broad meanings and narrow. These broad concepts of sacred are generally based on the inherent usefulness of the thing being seen as sacred. Things like the planet, water, air and fire are seen as sacred because we can't live without them. While it often pains us to say this, we use this definition with a vicious dichotomy. Water is sacred because we need it to live, but our cars or jobs, as creations of man are evil and therefore not sacred, whether we need them to live or not.

It is my view that a rational concept of All-That-Is as sacred involves not just the simple creations of the divine we generally see as sacred because of their usefulness but, yes, even things like cars and jobs that allow us to life in a way that is focused toward our true wills. Either all things have the capacity to be sacred or nothing has. We cannot say that just because we feel a person's sacred thing does not do what sacred things are supposed to do that it is not sacred. Indeed, sacredness can often be contrary. There are those who can see no knives or swords as sacred, while dozens of cultures label weapons sacred. I certainly find it difficult to see the sacred in the plain, concrete buildings that so many of the new local churches are in.

My wife is one of the hardest-working people I know — not because she goes to work at 6:00 every morning rain or shine — but because she recognizes each workday as part of the sacred assignment she has taken upon herself. She does not, as many others do, live for the weekend, nor spend the day looking at the clock. When, as has happened in the past, she finds herself with no work on her desk and hourly pay, she does not look for make-work. In fact, she has been known to go to her boss and tell him that it was not economically feasible for her to spend the rest of the day sitting around on his buck, so she would ask to leave for the day to save the company money and herself some time.

This isn't to say she's perfect; I've certainly been home, being the housewife, and received the call where she expresses frustration at her job or the waste of her time, especially if her next project involves waiting for an out-of-state coworker to send her materials, and she must literally sit in one place waiting. This can be especially aggravating as she is generally perceived as lightning-fast by her co-workers. I can only, I suppose, relate the similar feeling from elementary school where I, five levels above my nearest classmate, would literally dig my nails into my hand to prevent screaming out loud when a slow student had to read aloud. There was so much more I could be doing, but social structure made the only acceptable thing sitting there quietly and looking attentive.

This is not to say we understand her job to be sacred the same way that, say, the Holy Grail or Pope might be to other people. What we understand instead is a broad sacredness that includes all those things we need to live our lives, regardless of how those things came to be. Our houses, food, air, earth and heat are all equally sacred, and we recognize as sacred those things that, in addition to meeting our physical needs, also meet our emotional and social ones. She is not merely my wife but my sacred lover; our jobs are not mere sources of employment, but sacred battles we fight to further our causes — predominantly our family.

As powerful as this broad concept of sacred is, it is not really relevant to the topic of this section. Space may be sacred for no reason other than the fact that it fulfills a need, but the sacred space I will speak of in the next several sections is, instead, defined as sacred in the more traditional concepts of consecration and being set aside. These narrower definitions of sacred should be understood as related to, but not the same as, the concept of things being sacred merely by virtue of fulfilling a need.

That dichotomy is very difficult for a lot of people to understand, but I generally tell people the difference is between the concept of water as sacred and the difference between the general concept of "water" and a specific sacred body of water. A lake in which baptism occurs (if you recognize baptism as a rite) is somehow different from a puddle of water in the street, or water in a glass. A lake held as sacred by your people, that is prayed to or to which you make some kind of sacrifices to, or even an ocean that is told of in your myths as the birth waters of the human species, is not sacred because it is water. It is sacred because it is part of a greater body of mythology, and a greater part of your culture. This distinguishes the idea of sacred waters from water being sacred because we need it.

The Wiccan Temple: Sacred space of this world and not of it

The obvious first space to discuss in a Wiccan discussion of sacred spaces is the Temple, also called the circle[9]. We cast the circle in a number of different ways, all invested with the same main purpose: placing ourselves within a sacred space. The idea of what exactly this sacred space is varies from Wiccan to Wiccan. For some it is a literal marking upon the ground within which lies an area sanctified as surely as any room in a church. For others, the practice itself is a form of prayer, a set of movements that engage the body and mind in a sort of dynamic meditation, a set of cues and motions that tell the higher mind that now is the time to be involved.

This last definition is especially important because it is the true heart of the circle—it is a transformation as much within the self as without it. In Ceremonial Magic, the circle is used for containment, and usually the work is done outside of it, or sometimes outside of a central circle within a larger circle. In Wicca, the person creating the circle, whom I call by the imperfect name "the caster," is within the circle and contained by it. It makes a good metaphor, just as the Wiccan casts the circle from within and the mage casts it from without, the transformation for a Wiccan is within the Wiccan, and for a Magus is outside the Magus. This distinction is vital to an understanding of the differ-

---

[9] Casting the Circle falls into a collection of techniques known as "Erecting the Temple."

ence between the two, although the mechanism of this difference is up for debate.

The actual mechanics of the circle are unimportant to a discussion of the ideas of the sacred space within it, so we'll set them aside for the purposes of this work[10], and instead focus on the concepts of space within the circle. In general there are three types of circle space: the physical, the mental and the magical or energetic. The physical circle represents the actual position of the circle, traditionally marked out with salt, chalk, holy water, a line in the dirt or even paint. The concept in marking such a boundary is that the markings serve as notice both to the outside world and your higher mind or inner self that this space represents something more than the space outside it. In words, we say that no one is allowed within that space unless they come there of their own free will and with no ill intention.

Traditionally, it is said that this is the ancient aspect of the circle, and despite Wicca's state as a modern religion, it is in this place that the mythic history is partially correct. The uses of the circle as a protected or protective space speak to something deep inside of us. Even animals circle before sleeping, so drawing boundaries around our cities, even our houses, is something present in some form in most cultures. Again, this fascination likely speaks to a deep inner desire as well as the basic mechanical function of separating here and there.

More important than boundaries, to my mind, at least, is the use of the circle as a visual cue which uses accompanying memories to put the brain in the proper state for worship. In UEW, for example, the discussion of each element is accompanied by some form of guided meditation so that when the time comes for the use of, say, water, the UEWiccan has a genuine physical and mental knowledge of the element. Thus the elemental part of the Wiccan circle becomes a cycling through the mental states we associate with each element. This mental space-keeping is important, in my opinion, because it helps us to separate the spiritual activity in our being — a separation that aids in recognition of the spiritual and inevitably leads back to the will-

---

[10]It is, however, discussed *ad infinitum* in my forthcoming work, *The Circle, Cubed: Erecting the Temple in Four Dimensions.*

ing union of spiritual and nonspiritual. In other words, we learn to separate the spiritual from the nonspiritual so we can recombine them with what we deem a more appropriate focus.

Important to this mental idea is the concept of the circle as a space both in this world and outside it. To those who see Wiccan practice in terms of pure energy, this is a literal transformation, with some actually believing that the circle is a form of selective space/time transport. It is not surprising, then, that it is these people who most stringently associate the circle with the protective circles of Ceremonial Magic. Many of us are familiar, for example, with the wood cut "John Dee and his magical circle" in which the famous magician is portrayed in the center of a circle in a graveyard, speaking with a ghost. This woodcut was very influential in early Wicca, and I have in my possession a book with a press picture of Gerald Gardner working with essentially the same circle.

To those who believe that the circle is a space existing on the astral plane, in faerie or in another dimension, there is an obvious need for protection, since these places are supposedly filled with nasty boggles. This fear-based drive for the perfect circle, in my estimation, is the source for more strife and anxiety in the new Wiccan than fear of persecution or being seen as a weirdo. I have witnessed first-hand a teacher tell a student that he saw someone step outside a circle and vanish completely, never to be seen again. My ungracious response to this nonsense was to ask her the person's name, so I could check the status of the case and get the personal details before leading an astral plane rescue squad, but the "teacher" in question quickly changed her knowledge from something she'd seen to something she'd heard about, and promised to email me the name and police reports. This was over 5 years ago, and she still hasn't gotten back to me, not that I'm counting. I'm sure it's something on her extensive to-do list.

It is from these people we see the addition of elements of ceremonial magic to the circle — John Dee's inherently Christian watchtowers and angels, powdered sulfur, silver or iron, quicksilver (mercury) or blood, and the names of the Abrahamic deity. I find these things funky mood setters at best. They are to the Wiccan circle what a lava lamp is to a living room: tacky, funky, fun and something people may have to their heart's desire until they expect *me* to have it. My living room, 80% IKEA and 20%

yard sale, is tacky and funky enough, as is my circle! At the worst, however, these things become a distraction from the Wiccan's purpose for having the circle: communion with the divine, whether it be the outer divine, the inner, or both.

This leaves the energetic or magick nature of the circle. I use "magick" here, as opposed to magic, not because I think that magic-without-a-k will be confused with stage magic but because I speak of the same energy, the same intentional action, as Crowley did in his works, especially *Magick in Theory and Practice*. As I have said, I consider any other use of the word magick to be silly, and any spelling permutations beyond it to be extraordinarily pointless, so anytime I use the word "magick" with a k there is a reference to Crowley. That being said, this magical nature is to see the circle as an extension of the power of the Will, or the power of intention.

With that idea behind us we can understand the ideas behind the energetic notions of the circle. When not being used as a dynamic meditation it serves as a receptacle for the energy expressed as a form of the will. It is for this reason that some envision it a cone, sphere, or cylinder which can be selectively burst to direct one's power into the universe in the direction of desire. This is conceptualized by some in the form of prayer, in the form of excited molecules, even in the form of a gas-like aether which takes the magical energy and directs it to the designated place — towards a goal, towards generic goodness or to the gods themselves. In this use, the circle is as much a container as bowl or goblet, and therefore the boundaries, if not seen as completely impermeable, are at least seen as selectively so.

Regardless of the conceptualization or purpose, whether you see the outer edge of the circle as the gateway to another world or as the mental boundary between one type of experience and another, what cannot be denied is the innate holiness of the space. It is sanctified in the classical sense — set aside from normal usage. It is this idea of sanctification that leads to other notions of Wiccan sacred space, but is only the Wiccan circle that can be picked up and moved around as we see fit.

The Grove: An outdoor permanent sacred space

I'd like to take a break here and discuss a sacred space I am familiar with. In the southern edge of the Adirondacks somewhere, there lies a fence. Within that fence, an hour's walk from the road, is another fence. It is a serious fence, made of an environmentally-friendly recycled plastic that looks vaguely wood-like. This fence runs in a pentagon, about 50 feet along each side. To the casual hiker or hunter who ignores the outer fence, clearly marked "No Trespassing" and "Posted: No Hunting," this fence probably looks like yet another one of the many mystery sites we have in upstate New York, places where the wild raspberries and black caps are protected by people in military uniforms[11].

It looks this way on purpose, built by a marine with a good idea of what weirds people out. It seems out-of-place in a good way; you don't see it until you come up on it, but once you see it, it's impossible to miss. The tin plates stapled to the fence reading danger and no trespassing seem the same as you might find surrounding quicksand, or sinkholes or even worse things to step upon, so I suspect most people wouldn't feel compelled to step within the perimeter without a good reason. Certainly none of my readers, recognizing the fence from my descriptions, would bother the space, although inside I have to admit some small fear that someone will read this and decide to ignore a fence that genuinely hides some danger and get themselves killed, so — well, you've been warned.

Within this particular fence lies a small bit of forest, mostly maple, and a single glacial boulder, nearly perfectly white. Every three or four years, a group of people go out to this space, uproot any non-indigenous plants, check the other plants for diseases and go home. They do not perform any ritual, nor do they so much as speak an unneeded word within that boundary fence. That space is, in fact, a sacred grove.

I had the honor of being one of the people to do maintenance on it nearly a decade ago. To get there, we went down a "road" (actually, a fire break), scaled a steep embankment and avoided the den of a mother bear. We were eaten alive by mosquitoes, scraped ourselves on sharp rocks and went up to our knees in freezing water and mud. With hand axes, we chopped down an invasive species of maple outside the grove to protect the indigenous sugar maples, knowing a chainsaw would dis-

---

[11] Truth be told, everyone knows these spots for radar arrays, missile silos and testing facilities, but we pretend that these things are, in fact, not there, to preserve the illusion of military facilities as distant things we needn't think on often.

turb the birds nesting in the nearby trees. This was not a sort of new-age, passive-aggressive environmentalism, where you purchase land and ignore it in the hopes that the trees and weeds, left to their own devices, will be preferable to the use another may have for the land. Instead it was an active participation in maintaining the land in a pristine state. Nature is left to its own devices with the understanding that mankind can, in fact, disguise himself as nature. A gorgeous Norway Maple[12], for example, as it exterminates the plant life beneath it one plant at a time, may look like a beautiful landscaping device, but with its many seeds, which can travel a significant distance from the mother plant, it is nearly as bad a critter as the plants we typically imagine as invasive: honeysuckles, ivies, and kudzu.

This grove, lovingly created by a Pagan who happens to be in the business of wildlife management, is the best of the environmentally sensitive and the sacred. It reflects the earliest of ideas of sacred and of sacrifice—the act of setting something aside for a thing bigger than you. This land is, in fact, sacrosanct, impossible or at least extremely difficult for the state to seize. As a thriving grove of indigenous trees and plants, including three endangered and one threatened species, should it ever leave the hands of the manager and his family, it would still be very difficult to destroy with the public's attention (not to mention just difficult to get to, surrounded as it is by a low floodplain full of biting insects.)

This sacred space is not a worship space in the classical sense, where people meet to hold rituals and have prayers. This sacred space is worshipped by being maintained and cared for. While it is true we girdled every Norway maple we saw traveling there, and treated a few trees for fungi, lest they spread to the grove, we understood that the forestland here was too big to be maintained by a small group of people and made the conscious decision to focus on this one protected area, filling in blanks where possible but otherwise leaving the forest around it

[12] As I was writing this, I realized Norway maples were still being sold as ideal shade trees, despite the efforts of people like me.
http://www.hort.uconn.edu/cipwg/art_pubs/docs/norway_maple.pdf provides some information on the plant.

to fend for itself. This serves two basic purposes: it serves to produce valuable oxygen without doing damage to the land around it, and by creating an indigenous environment; it allows the preservation of that environment—which, of course, is spreading. Already the sugar maples are filling in the area around the grove, and the last time an acquaintance of mine served clean-up duty there, a huge hive of feral honeybees was nesting in and around the fence[13]. He also saw signs of raptors in the area.

The fact that plants can do damage to the land around them is unknown by many people. An example of passive-aggressive environmentalism gone wrong happened a few years ago in Michigan when a family's purchase of old commercial land lead to an unmaintained orchard that was left to its own devices for ten years and inevitably got infected with a number of diseases and pests—diseases and pests that crept over fences to commercial orchards. The family, who were fans of the environment, was distraught that they were ordered to treat or remove the trees, viewing their land, which had sprouted many indigenous plants and attracted wildlife, as a boon to the environment instead of a menace. In their view, it had reverted to a natural state, but in reality, it was only a pest both to commercial farmers and indigenous plant preservationists. Whenever an animal ate their windfall fruit and moved on to other lands, hardy non-indigenous apple trees sprouted, and what indigenous plants were on their land were threatened by being a part of an environment they are not a part of naturally, and could do so much better and thrive if the non-indigenous apples were replaced (even if by other apple trees)!

Since many equate Wicca with environmentalism, despite the fact that it's not an original aspect of the religion, it is important to many Wiccans to be environmentally active. Environmental activity can involve, as I have said in the past, nothing

[13] Wild honeybees are endangered in the wild in that area, mostly because of a parasite. From what I understand, this particular hive was studied by a local university by request of the land managers, but the mechanics of that investigation and the outcome are not known to me. I do know that the landowners drilled holes in the fence to encourage other bees. It is a—pardon the pun—sticky situation for those wanting to keep indigenous spaces. Honeybees are not indigenous to North America, but most of the feral bees fill a needed niche here.

more than setting aside land for the production of oxygen and the benefits of greenspace, or setting it aside as a special place not for human contact, or for minimal human contact. However, this consecrated land cannot be allowed to be harmful to the land around it or destructive in general, and that means having an active participation in the land that is set aside, even if, as it was in many ancient religions, the land is preserved for the gods, not for man.

The Temple: Permanent sacred spaces for the act of worship or honor

More accessible in our minds, perhaps, is the idea of the temple, a sacred space, indoors or out, set up to revere a deity or as a place for worship. They come in two basic types, those that house cult statues or relics and those used as worship spaces. This first type I generally refer to as shrines, because the small forest altars and household shrines we are most familiar with are easy-to-imagine examples. However, many of the greatest temple remains from the ancient past fall into this category: places that housed relics or images of the gods, or of a particular god, where one might visit to stand in awe or offer a sacrifice, but not places where one would enter for communal worship.

The most visible of this type of temple is probably The Parthenon, which housed a great cult statue of Athena. Although the space had later been used for a church and a mosque, the original intention was not a building one entered to do those things many westerners equate with worship. These things, such as going into the building in large numbers, listening to a person give a sermon or speech and singing, praying and doing other types of worship *within* the building, are reserved for the second kind of temple, the communal one.

These shrines, while not serving as places for huge group worship, have a valuable position in reality. Where visible, they send the brain a reminder of the visibility of the gods in our lives. One metaphor I am fond of is that temples to the gods in visible places, whether a startlingly large monument at the highest point of your city or a small, bright shrine centrally placed in your house, serve to remind us of the gods in the same way that trees remind us of the wind. When we cannot feel or hear the wind, the movement of the trees reveals its presence, and in those times when we cannot feel or hear the gods, the presence of shrines reveals their presence, or at least reminds us of times when we felt their presence enough to build shrines to them.

I genuinely believe that a spiritual life is a combination of spiritual practice and living in such a way that the spiritual is always just under the surface of your consciousness. I believe we can be trained to interpret visual cues to the divine as clearly as we can learn to pick up body language and that training our minds to snap to awareness of the divine when needed can open up a whole new range of thought. We find ourselves with expanded minds that require no drugs or deceptions to grow, just deity.

This is a pretty rigid theological position from a former atheist, admittedly, but it factors into a core part of my view of the divine, and that of Wicca, that if something is so unbelievable to you that it elicits a powerful negative response, it is wrong for you to follow or honor that something. The other side of this coin, the part relevant to the ideas of temples and shrines, is that if something elicits a powerful positive response, you are obligated to pursue it. We bring religion out of the stratosphere of superego and higher mind and come down to the animal mind—rats in a Skinner box, pressing the levers that give us food or pleasure, and avoiding the ones that bring us pain and sickness. At the same time as we are like these poor, tortured rats, we understand the higher mind's ability to mediate our responses, and we are thinking like real human beings. We know for a fact that we can deal with extraordinary pain when it is for a higher purpose, and that the higher mind can alleviate the most visceral responses. Therefore, a truly visceral response is a reaction both of the higher mind and the animal one.

This is, however, not a part of one of my neuroscience lectures, and tangential to the discussion at hand, so I will bring this back on topic by saying only that people who have experienced these gut sensations of the presence of the divine crave them as much as our bodies crave oxygen and food, and therefore it is only natural that they do those things that elicit such responses as much and as often as possible. With that in mind, it becomes obvious that the search for communion with the divine, even the minute communion of being reminded of their presence, can be embodied in the viewing of shrines and temples.

With that out of the way, we can discuss the second type of temple structures, which can range from what we generally think of as temples — giant edifices of marble and stone — to a simple ring made from trees in a field. These structures, regardless of their formality, are temples that serve the same purpose as the churches we may be more familiar with: a place for communal worship. Their permanence serves a different purpose than the rite of the circle casting, which represents a sort of personal space at one moment in time. The permanent temple serves as a community meeting area that allows the community to better describe itself: "We are the coven that meets at the Black Oak Sanctuary on Fourth Street."

In the early days of Wicca the temple or large shrine was something that existed only in the domain of the rich eccentric, or existed on private property, perhaps well-liked by the community but still the possession of the landholders. With the larger groups of today's Wicca, especially urban groups, the idea of building permanent community worship space is not only in the hands of the general populace, but something that becomes possible with a minimum of investment in a community. In many cities, an older two story building on the outskirts of a commercial district can be rented for less than $500/month, owned for even less, and a community of only 100 people who actively contribute a small amount to the building fund are fully capable of keeping it running if they have some form of leadership and active organization. Such buildings are almost always historical, in need of preservation and on bus routes, so the positive energy and feasibility of such an endeavor is obvious.

Regretfully, the petty infighting and nonsensical actions of some "leaders" in the Pagan community are so off-putting that we have a significant number of people who will probably never trust any leader, no matter how skilled. In addition, the behavior of some independent Pagans towards people they perceive as leaders can be so similarly inane that a significant percentage of otherwise excellent leaders simply haven't the Teflon coating needed to put up with it. Those groups that can find more than fifty people to work together are often fairly insular, which is not what a broad-based community temple really needs, but serves a purpose nonetheless — as an example of what not to do.

If we imagine for a moment we have a group of about one hundred people in a depressed urban area willing to participate in a communal temple, we can see right away the right way to go about it: an area dedicated to a god, a pantheon or worship itself, overseen by people invested in its upkeep, but still a public service. Statues, meeting rooms, places of worship are placed as needed by the community and perhaps the endeavor is funded by a small shop or by lending rooms out for gaming groups, support groups, classes and meetings. One gaming organization who took a similar approach found that by having vending machines with snacks and sodas they not only funded their space but brought in funds from people in a nearby office building, which had only one high-priced vending machine.

If the community is large enough to fund the living quarters and a small stipend for a full time clergyperson, who is essentially being paid to be available at all times, more power to them. Likewise, if the community finds itself too small to afford the space alone, and can share it with a similarly minded community, that has worked in the past as well. These "next generation" temples serve the purpose of the marketplaces or meadhalls of our ancestors. They are places where the community meets in the real world to interact, worship and learn. My own marriage was the result of similar networking, so I obviously advocate it fully.

In my opinion, these community centers/temples are the direction of the Wicca of the next twenty years. Too many otherwise great examples of them are ruined by being affiliated with shops with questionable ethics, or with insular groups, or power-hungry leaders and burned out community members, but those few that survive will pave the way for an ease of access to communal worship that would shock and amaze Wicca's founders.

The Wicca of the far future... intentional communities?

I have often described Wicca as the state-religion of the micronation of Wiccans, a sort of macroscopic faith of large rituals and broad points of view within which there exist numerous subgroups, cults, covens, individuals and families. From this point of view, the position of the pan-traditional temple is an obvious one, and the flaw of allowing one sect to possess it clear.

However, it also indicates the possibility for an even better form of communal worship: the intentional community.

If a single person has more reason to mistrust intentional communities than I, I pity them. I describe myself as a misanthrope but in fact I am a rarer creature known as the demonstrative introvert. Put bluntly, people exhaust me. When I have attended a social function I have to decompress alone, maybe before my computer, with a white noise generator in the room and headphones blaring music, for a minimum of two hours before I feel better. Better yet, I take a long shower and a nap, preferably not at the same time. I don't know how I came to be this way, as my childhood was punctuated by my mom's circle of social contacts. Many events that I prefer to keep to myself, like birthdays and holidays, were, in my childhood, full of people.

It's obviously not an environmental phenomenon, as my son is very much the same way, despite a radically different childhood. I'm not sure it is not genetic, either, as my family tree is punctuated by weirdoes and even the occasional agoraphobic. It is different from agoraphobia because it is not a fear of or anxiety over people, just a need for space away from them and a need to meet with them on my terms. I have no issues when I am giving a lecture or tour, running a game or sport or leading a teaching circle, and I did fine with my own teacher, who recognized my need for space and tended to keep me working in pairs and trios, rather than with the whole coven, whenever possible.

It is perhaps surprising then, that I have lived on two communes, two other environments that could've been called communes without stretching the term too far, and have had some of my best life experiences on an intentional community. It is less surprising that some of my worst, most heart wrenching experiences occurred in the same types of places. This affords me the unique ability to look at intentional community life and evaluate what truly works.

The most effective intentional community that I have been a part of, even if only very briefly, was the one from which the UEW tradition arose. It worked because it reflected an understanding that, just as people have different learning styles, people have different living styles. The six buildings used exclusively for living space included a house with twelve people, each sharing a bedroom with two others, and a larger house in which a single person lived, with three guest bedrooms, and an office. In the range between these extremes were other buildings which held families in varying stages of communal structure. Each house was valued by the community in terms of square feet and the amount of dollars or labor dollars (an amount of money "earned" for working on the land, doing chores, tending the garden, etc) per square foot was divided amongst the residents of the house in a manner of their choosing. Since several of the members of the community worked outside the community and paid in money, instead of labor, the community worked well until it was amicably dissolved when the cost of living in the area began to exceed the reach of most members. Some went off to start new communes in other places while others, me included, went to live "normal" lives.

What made this community work—beyond sharing an economic philosophy that allowed those not inclined towards manual labor to pay into the community with dollars, and allowed those who found holding traditional jobs difficult, but weren't afraid of hard work, to pay in labor—was respect for the spaces of other people. There were communal spaces and private ones, spaces for families to keep together and spaces to work and meet with others. People respected the invisible boundaries between them. Most importantly, there were shared spaces for worship and community gathering, which gave us a sense of unity even when we were apart.

It is this direction I see Wicca beginning to take in twenty or thirty years, toward intentional communities, focused around sects or traditions that use a more rational concept of community than many communes do, and have a variety of living types and topographies: urban intentional communities, taking up floors of previously abandoned warehouses, rural intentional communities involved in agriculture or distance technologies, and everything in-between.

I do not see such communities as theocracies, and indeed would find it odd for the spiritual leader and community leader to be the same person, as any spiritual leader would need to be primarily sensitive to the spiritual needs of the people and a community leader would need to be business savvy. For example, it is unlikely a community would pay the rent of someone who regularly went through periods of "bad energy" and refused to work, even though it would be a spiritual leader's obligation to help work them through it, even if only to get them appropriate counseling. Your priestess' name on an eviction notice would be pretty awful.

What I do see is adults deciding to live and raise families around people with similar values, both as a form of networking and as a form of protection from radical Abrahamicists, who have made it clear they do not wish to cohabit with us. If worse comes to worst, these communities can provide a limited form of safety in numbers and shelter from fundamentalism should the radicals painting the Christianity of the future as gun-toting lunatics prove Cassandras despite our skepticism. Unless the laws of most western countries are gutted, private property in the future will still have more protection than public property and intentional communities with land owned by a single person or by a co-op will have the right to keep proselytes off their property with impunity.

The thin line here is evident: we can become so insular that we become as bad as those who mean to do us harm. However, as a mom whose son has described an outright fear of Christians despite his experiences, not because of them, and who constantly has to hear a list of the good ones in his life from his parents, I must admit that the safety of a place where I can send my son to the playground and not worry about his coming back with a Bible and a fear of Hell appeals to me. Likewise, I'd like to know that I could place a statue of Apollo in my backyard and know that there was nothing a neighbor could do (or would want to do) about it.

If we go that route, and I personally hope we do, the ability to build community structures, worship spaces, libraries, even swimming pools, becomes more feasible. In addition, we gain the ability to set the key for our families and our lives in such a way that attunement with the divine, even if it leads to a faith we wouldn't personally choose, is a foremost part of a person's life. We can choose to not link things like respect for differences and love of education and truth to religious values, and instead see them as community values, thus changing the world for the better one group at a time.

Recommended Reading for Topic Sixteen:

http://www.ic.org/

Discussion Questions for Topic Sixteen:

16.1. What is the difference between something that is sacred for fulfilling a need and other types of sacred?

16.2. What are some of the purposes of the circle?

16.3. What conceptualizations of the Wiccan circle appeal to you? Why?

16.4. What is the purpose of setting aside land for the use of the land?

16.5. What is meant by "Passive-Aggressive Environmentalism?"

16.6. How would an outdoor Temple be different from a grove using the distinctions in the chapter?

16.7. What distinction is being made between a Temple and a Shrine?

16.8. Why do some community temples fail while others excel?

16.9. What are the benefits and flaws of intentional community living?

Wicca in Practice V: Evaluating and Recognizing Propaganda.

"It's only propaganda when it is the other side; when we agree, it is inspirational literature!"

Introduction

One of the strengths of a historically interpretive tradition is that most members spend a great deal of time contemplating the manner in which they fit into the world. They accept that each individual will have a different interpretive framework based upon his or her own perceptions. This is in contrast to one of the weaknesses of strictly prescribed belief systems: that most adherents haven't thought as much about the manner in which they fit into the world as they have about discovering the rules of their system so they'll know what to believe and how to behave. It is not a path of discovery; it is a path of rote. It is the difference between learning to repeat what someone has said to you, and learning to understand it. Both modes, however, are vulnerable to propaganda.

Calling an item of literature or speech propaganda is a good way to get people to assume you dislike it and disagree with you because of your alleged feelings. They make the assumption that propaganda is a subjective thing, that we can't recognize it when we see it and that the use of the term to describe anything is just opinion. In reality, such statements cannot be further from the truth: propaganda is an easily definable thing: it is literature, speech or similar media designed to make you agree with the author or hold the intended point-of-view without thinking too hard about it.

Some of our greatest pieces of literature are propaganda. *Les Miserables*, The Aeneid, The Declaration of Independence, even Kennedy's "Ask not what your country can do for you" speech all have moments of propagandizing. The first two instances are extreme, because both works were designed to cause subtle changes in their readers' emotions toward a political regime, and to put the recent turmoil in their countries of origin in perspective. The similarity between the two is more extreme in their original languages, but even with the worst translations you can pick up the similarities.

I despise hidden propaganda when I find it, and have even deleted hundreds of thousands of words that I have written that I knew were just too divisive and geared towards emotion. I have trained myself, over years, to try to point out my biases and prejudices whenever they may be creeping up in a discussion and to admit where I am not objective. It was never an easy task, but I facilitated it by studying the masters of propaganda... not just Virgil and Hugo but Capra, quite possibly the greatest of American propagandists, and most of our modern politicians. I have a gift of being able to manipulate words and phrases effectively and use them for my own devices. (Just ask my wonderful Latin and Roman culture professor, who once received two essays from me that used the same exact materials to describe Augustus as the best and worst thing that ever happened to Rome.) Phoenix has said often that were I devoid of moral backbone I could make a fortune as a televangelist, and there have been times I have contemplated doing it only to show people what deceptive crackpots evangelist leaders are, but I know too many people would be hurt and therefore the possible good effects outweigh the negative.

People who are familiar with this "skill" of mine sometimes revel in it. I get forwarded emails and pointed at message boards when people have lost the ability to argue with someone because they are being manipulative. My friends know that I can handle it and that I consider such things practice for my art. I have a personal journal full of refutations of people like Robertson, Bush and Gingrich, folk who wouldn't give me the time of day but whose intensely ignorant comments warranted refutation nonetheless. These things are practice, of course, for the day I become an evil dictator and everyone has to do as I say.

Now, before I go on, I must admit another bias. This section here was supposed to be about logical fallacy, not about propaganda. I can look to my left, to the space on my hands-free paper holder where an outline with the phrase "Wicca in Practice V: Logical Fallacies" is typed with a line through it, a handwritten URL and one long phrase (which came after my wife and I got in another fight over this stupid, stupid Iraq war). "Why is it that when Bush uses the stories of killed Kurds and victimized Iraqis it is being manipulative and when Starhawk writes "In Nablus on the Eve of War," which uses the death of Rachel Corrie the *exact* same way, it's just calling our attention to the tragedy of war?"

The phrase beneath it, which made Phoenix and I smile tragically, and really brought an end to the row, is the phrase that starts this section: "It's only propaganda when it is the other side. When we agree, it is inspirational literature!"

Let me get back to me for a second. My reactions to propaganda come in two distinct forms. In the more common reaction, I hear or read it, recognize it for what it is and laugh or groan about it. It bugs me that people fall for it, but since I don't, and most of it is harmless manipulation of a group of people choosing to be manipulated I forget about it and move on. The second reaction, and less common, is a primitive, painful gut reaction. It occurs when I read or otherwise experience propaganda and don't realize that I've been manipulated by it until afterwards (or halfway through.) Such reactions make me physically ill, the cognitive dissonance I experience generally translated into a stomach ache or a migraine. In part, it is sheer ego, I am so disgusted that I, who (like all people) think of myself as above the common idiot, could be tricked into feeling what someone wants me to feel, that I make myself physically ill.

I am convinced that these reactions are utterly psychosomatic, but like Spiderman's spider sense, there have been times where the nausea came before I realized I was falling for the propaganda, clueing me into the fact that even as my conscious mind was going along with the manipulation, part of me was not falling for it. For the most part, these propaganda reactions are most intense when two criteria are met. For the first criterion, I must feel that the author is skilled enough to know better, which means that s/he was writing with the intention of manipulating people, and with the full knowledge of the effects of the effort. In other words, it occurs when what I am reading is intentional propaganda or the work of someone so blinded by the belief that s/he was correct that s/he felt that the manipulation was fair play. The second criterion for a strong negative reaction to propaganda is when I *know* that the person writing it is morally superior to what he or she has written — or at least has claimed to be.

I mentioned Starhawk's "In Nablus on the Eve of War" earlier because it was that article that put the line through "Logical

Fallacies" and turned this into "Evaluating and Recognizing Propaganda"... and set me on a new journey. In part, this journey is about my generation of Pagans, the under-represented "middle generation" who fell into Wicca between the small boom in Paganism in the 1970s and the huge one in the 1990s. We are a pretty battered group, many of whom started Wiccan and left Wicca for more rational groups, and we don't have that many idols. What idols we do have are generally held in proper esteem. We don't think them gods on earth. We point out to our students where they are wrong and where they are right, but we generally think of them as pretty stand-up individuals. I can no longer number Starhawk amongst those individuals, as a result of this nasty turn in her politics, the events of June 2001 and a number of other small things that individually mean nothing but taken collectively are too problematic to ignore.

Recognizing and evaluating propaganda

That rather painful introduction over, we can get to what propaganda is and how to deal with it. Propaganda is, as I said, literature or other media designed to make you agree with a desired point of view, preferably without thinking too hard about it. It accomplishes this in a number of ways, some of them unethical, others only unethical when hidden.

In general, the difference between propaganda and inspirational media is not really whether or not we agree with it but how hidden the manipulation of the person experiencing the medium is. Frank Capra, for example, is considered by many America's finest propagandist. He wrote and created a number of propaganda films for the US government, and used these techniques in his Hollywood pictures. While it is not the best example of his work, most of us are familiar with *It's a Wonderful Life*, which uses many of these techniques to swell us into a holiday mood of "No matter how bad it gets, it's good to be alive!"

George Bailey is everything we like to see ourselves as. More than three quarters of the movie is set-up for the last twenty minutes or so when George meets an angel, loses his previous life, gets it back, and lives happily ever after. If you watch just the last quarter of the movie, never having seen the rest, it is incredibly annoying, preachy and unlikely. If, however, you allow yourself to become sympathetic to George Bailey, through means like the selective back and forth between third person and third person omniscient the beginning is told in, and the use of soliloquy, sympathy and appeal to the common man the film uses, the ending seems wonderful and heartbreaking. I love the movie. I cry every time I watch it like a sap. I allow myself to be swept up in the mastery of the whole thing. It's highly cathartic despite the fact that it speaks to none of my experiences. I'm the same way with A Christmas Carol, and Merry Christmas, Charlie Brown, so knowing propaganda is there doesn't mean you can't choose to be affected by it at times.

The difference between these things and the propaganda that bothers me is that I know, when watching a holiday movie, that I'm being manipulated toward a certain feeling. I make the decision to accept or reject that manipulation. Propaganda hidden in the news, or in the voices of our spiritual leaders, is much more insidious. Should we really doubt and fear our leaders every time they speak and trust nothing anyone says? That's no way to live, frankly.

The good thing about propaganda is that we can train ourselves to recognize it at an intuitive level. Propaganda uses subtle indicators to let you know that it is there. When you can spot these things, you can spot the propaganda. Once you have this ability, you can choose to be affected by it or not. This informed decision allows you to draw rational conclusions about information.

The easiest indicator that something is a bit more than it seems is your own reaction to it. If the material you read creates strong emotions in you, it is likely that it was intended to do so. It is up to you to figure out if those emotions were the intended ones or not. For example, if I read an article by Pat Robertson saying that Christianity is dwindling in America's schools and proposing a new mission to put an end to that, I'm going to be livid, but I know that my reaction—one of general shock and disgust at fringe Christianity's attempt to coerce people's kids into Christianity—would not be what he intended. Indeed, my reaction, which would involve trying to find if these fringe groups were involved in my local schools, would be the exact opposite of his intention.

However, to use the example in the introduction, when I read Starhawk's unfair attempt to link the death of Rachel Corrie with what the US was doing in Baghdad, my initial response—

anger at both Corrie's death and the impending war — was *exactly* what the article was supposed to cause. That anger clued me in that something was wrong. Being emotionless was not what I would expect, but to get angry and depressed at one group of people for something done by another did not make sense, and it was that lack of sense that got the warning signals going and my brain looking for answers.

The incident above is a good example of transference, one of the propagandist's easiest to use tools. We see this when a war protester is accused of not remembering the World Trade Center, even when what they are protesting has nothing to do with that incident. It is the unfair linking of something that creates justifiable emotion — pride, anger, resentment, outrage, happiness — with something totally unrelated to it or, at best, tangentially related to it.

We see this on television all the time. In a commercial in wide play locally, a doctor tells the story of his mother being trapped at home and having to go to a nursing home after a fall, something that could've been prevented with the use of his product. We must ask questions of ourselves when we hear this. Why is it so important that they tell us this guy is a doctor? Why is he wearing a lab coat for a commercial — is he afraid he'll get splattered with something? Why, in addition to telling us he's a doctor, wearing a lab coat and more do they also make sure to write that he's a doctor on the screen?

The answer here is that they are linking the respectability of a doctor's advice with the usefulness of the product. No indication is made that this product is preferable to similar devices, or to alternate methods of communicating, and there is no mention of the fact that anyone of any age could fall and be stuck at home without someone coming to their aid. Those things are unimportant; doctor says you need this product, and doctor represents respect and intelligence, therefore you need the product.

This can be done in terrifying ways. Nazi Germany linked nationalism, rational science and religion with the persecution of the Jews. David Koresh used the belief that being persecuted meant Christians were holy to get away with doing tons of things that warranted persecution. People have used and abused science, religion and other things to make their points for years without any hesitation.

To a degree, this is acceptable. If your religion teaches that you are not to eat meat, it is only reasonable that any argument you made for being a vegetarian be linked with your religion. Far too often, however, there is no linkage. Homosexuality, for example, is not in the Bible, but fringe Christians feel free to link it with things like the sin of Sodom (abuse of the stranger) and prohibitions against male prostitutes, even going so far as to label it a sin when the Bibles clearly have two types of prohibition — sins and breaking the cleanliness code — and what few verses can be logically read to include homosexuality place it in the same category as wearing a cotton/polyester blend shirt!

Another pair of examples, described in 333, is linking the acceptance of the theory of Evolution with the denial of Christianity, and linking any religion other than one's own with the worship of Satan. These false linkages seek to use the emotions one thing creates and "borrow" them for another thing, which is a very different creature than the use of religion, science or other criteria to discuss a relevant point.

The doctor example uses two types of erroneous linkage. One is caused by the borrowed respect of a doctor to the product and the other is a testimonial, a personal story that may actually be quite bizarre and unlikely but is true or presented as true, and makes the person hearing it think "What if that happened to me?" Testimonials are the favorite of politicians of the past three elections: I speak of behalf of Mary so-and-so, (who may not exist) a soccer mom who raised four children while staying at home and developing a cure for shower mildew! A testimonial can be accurate or not, legitimately connected to the situation or not and even sometimes just have nothing to do with what's being discussed. At times, testimonials are extrapolated into case studies, which sometimes but not always speak to broader situations. The good news regarding testimonials is that most of us can see when their use is justified or when they are just being abused.

Another type of borrowed emotion can come from using a word that is affiliated with a particular mode of behavior. If I describe myself as thrifty, it is different than being described as tightfisted, even though they mean similar things. Words like liberal, conservative, nazi, fascist, feminist and radical are all commonly used in pejorative ways. Every time you hear these and other words, the propaganda filters should kick on. Are these words being used manipulatively?

Another technique from the propagandist's workbook is the use of logical fallacies and appeals to a special (and sometimes fictional) audience. These are interrelated, so they can be discussed together without too much confusion. Fallacies include things we've talked about already — the false linking of one thing to another, as well as inappropriate conclusions, sweeping generalizations and, well, the grab bag of other things that just make no sense.

An example of this last category that comes to mind was my recent experience with a person who mistrusted Wicca because it was only 50 years old. A good way to see if something holds water is to apply it to other situations: would you mistrust a doctor with only 50 years or experience? How about a school? Is a high school that is 50 years old better than the one built last year? Cars? Computers? Meditation techniques? You can see the fallacy right away. Only religion was judged by this category, and the reason why was nothing but simple prejudice. There is a reasonable fear of those things that are brand new and untested, but as Wicca moves into the 4th and 5th generations of practitioners it's not exactly an untested phenomenon!

At the end of this book, in Appendix C, is a list of common logical fallacies, which a large quantity of propaganda consists of. The problem is that an inability to reason logically may not be propaganda, but simple idiocy. George Bush Jr., for example, frequently reaches mind-boggling conclusions, but my wife and I just don't agree on why. She tends to see his conclusions as propaganda whereas I just find him mind-numbingly stupid. The line between propaganda and stupidity, when it comes to logical fallacy, is often highly subjective. For me, if the emotional reaction is just outrage that someone who apparently graduated from high school at some point is incapable of forming a rational argument, rather than fears that I'm being manipulated, I tend to place it under the mental heading of idiocy.

Of course, this can be racked up to the fact that I am probably under the category of what George Bush Jr. would call the intellectual elite or the liberal left. (Hear that clicking? That's your propaganda filters coming on!) I'm generally considered well educated, if not over-educated. My education ranges from classical history and languages to the very foundations of existence: from evolution to the genetic code. Another tool propagandists often use is painting anyone of an opposing view who is generally considered educated—whether that is a personal consideration or the opinion of your enemies—as a diabolical figure skulking about in the shadows, perhaps like The Brain, the swollen-headed cartoon lab mouse whose nightly task is "the same thing we do every night, Pinky—try to take over the world!"

When Bush makes appeals to people who define themselves in ways other than by their education, sometimes called appeals to the common man, or even appeals to the unwashed, he is using the technique of special appeal. In general, there are four common special appeals. The first and most common is the appeal to the common man, either by casting the enemy as the over-educated, or as rich, privileged or otherwise empowered. The second is appeal to authority, such as invoking the fact that you speak for, or on behalf of, people with power over the lives of your audience, but also the appeal to what authority your audience has, i.e.: "It is up to you, the voters, to do what must be done and..." The third, and most obvious, in my opinion, is the appeal to the use of force, both in the blatant form of "Vote for me or I'll beat you up" and "Protest the war and you'll get fired," and also in the more subtle forms, such as "If this crime bill is not passed, I would not go outside the door unless you like being raped and mugged."

The last, and the ones we as religious individuals should be most careful of, is the appeal to deity—both in the form of speaking on behalf of deity and speaking to people as if they would agree with you if they spoke with their deity. "Look inside your heart! God has a message there for you! You, too, can support a child for only 80 cents a day! What does God tell you to do?" Some forms of these appeals are easily neglected. When a televangelist tells you his god says to send him money, few of us believe him. When you're a cancer victim suffering in the hospital, watching religious television on one of the four channels that your room's television gets, and the predatory minister claims that he's talking to YOU, fighting cancer in your hospital room all alone, no family near you, it doesn't matter that you're an inevitable demographic for daytime television, it seems as if he really is speaking to you, personally and, under the effects of drugs and stress, you may respond to him.

Other forms of logical manipulation, like sweeping generalizations, errors in correlation and false conclusions are fairly easy to see through if you just take the time to ask where these facts are coming from. That is the single tool that works against propaganda better than anything — asking questions. If someone says *all the people* are doing something, or *everyone* agrees, ask yourself if it is at all likely that even one person is outside this point of view? Probably! If someone says "Of course *you and I* know otherwise," ask yourself how this person knows you know otherwise? Is this a rational conclusion? If someone says people are out to get them from jealousy, anger or fear, ask yourself if this person has some magical ability to read emotions! In short, if you learn the questions to ask, and when to ask them, you can become aware of an entire new subtext to human communication and decide how and why you wish to participate in it.

Practice:

Evaluate the following statements. What forms of propaganda, if any, are being used?

"You know that Wicca is wrong. Jesus knows that Wicca is wrong. Ask Jesus what the real story is and you will find out."

"How can you say that you don't believe in hell? The problem with you is that you hate Christians!"

"If they don't change the directions they are flying on the broomsticks in the Harry Potter Movie, my powerful curse will cripple the movie's box office draw!"

"I support all the heroes who are bravely going out there to fight the war our President has justly proclaimed. I cannot understand how anyone who lives in this country, who faced September 11th, could do otherwise!"

"It doesn't matter if the war is just or unjust, let's all pray the soldiers come home safe!"

For further practice, just try watching the next speech by your favorite politician or 15 minutes of religious television.

Recommended Reading:

http://www.starhawk.org/activism/activism-writings/nablus.html

http://www.propagandacritic.com/

Topic Seventeen: Ásatrú

Our friends, the Northern Logosians

In *Wicca 333*, we spoke a lot about the Logosians, a fictional modern people much abused by the modern Pagan populace. In 333, we spoke predominantly of the effects of this modern Pagan populace on the Celts. This and the next three topics deal with four other real peoples similarly abused: Druids, Indigenous Americans, believers in Karma and the Ásatrú. Similar sections for the PA Dutch, Appalachian and Italian hereditary magical traditions are well-deserved, but as the groups I am discussing are often misrepresented by the passing along of mounds of poor information and lies by many, and the PA Dutch and Italian FMTs have been largely misrepresented by a very small handful of people, I would rather focus on those for whom lies and slander are the result of many people profiteering and others following along, not a select few greedy individuals who are better questioned on their ethics than corrected.

The followers of Ásatrú, specifically, have been disrespected by the Modern Wiccan community enough to make many of them distrustful of even the least biased Wiccan attempts to describe their faith to knowledge-hungry Wiccans. This is a shame, since even those Wiccans who grow out of the persecution complex are quick to help an abused ally, and many of the religious freedom groups most likely to rise to the assistance of an abused Ásatrúar[14] were founded by Wiccans. I would be lying if I said that I did not occasionally receive resistance and obnoxious behavior when I requested information. Many people simply have no clue that Wiccans exist beyond the 101 level, nor grasp that

---

[14] I will use the word Ásatrúar to mean the Icelandic Âsatrúarmaðr, which is a common convention. It essentially means a follower of Ásatrú, and herein will mean a member of the greater religion. According to http://www.irminsul.org/arc/011ht.html, from which the Icelandic word above comes, it is occassionally pluralized as Ásatrúars, but this has not been the experience of my research and I will go with what I hope is the more common use of Ásatrúar to mean both singular and plural. Whenever importing words into English, we must attempt to go with the conventions established by predecessors. I am aware of dissatisfaction with some of these conventions within the Ásatrú community, and for that reason am being explicit when I am bowing to a majority usage.

any liberal polytheistic religion that is based in respect for others simply must have a small knowledge of the native followers of various deities. How on earth are we to move through a multi-cultural society without a knowledge of those cultures? Without that knowledge, we are not just the bull in the china shop that many Wiccans are, but instead we are that bull with the addition of a blindfold.

That being said, I must admit a small fear here. When I describe Ásatrú in this section, I hope that none of *my* readers would use the information I provide to "flavor" their Wicca with Ásatrú terms and phrases. I present this information here not to provide spices that you can add to Wicca, but to provide alternate information to what you may find commonly discussed, with the goal that you, the reader, better understand a separate religion often lumped in with Wicca. These sections should give you information that may, in fact, lead you away from Wicca. If you read the material on Ásatrú and finds it resonates with you in a way that Wicca does not, I would hope you would have the courage to recognize that maybe a change in religion is in order. Wicca cannot be all things to all people or it ceases to make sense. It is not impossible that you will read this, come to the realization that you are an Ásatrúar and that this will be the last book on Wicca you ever read. This is a possibility that happens whenever Wiccan authors are not afraid to discuss religions in their proper context, and may be one excuse why other authors tell half-truths when discussing the Pagans and Heathens next door.

That being said, I'd like to remind my readers that the other things discussed thus far are still in effect. I will not remind people throughout this section that when I say the Ásatrú beliefs are polytheistic that I mean they are polytheistic, not followers of a great one God with archetypes or faces. Similarly, I will not go about re-explaining the ethics of calling people something they would not call themselves, nor will I redefine the terms religion or faith as meaning anything besides a relationship with the divine and a set of mores. I have had the rare honor of meeting many of my readers face to face and I know that you are all quite intelligent and do not need constant reminding! Indeed, the only reason I mention these things at all is for the sake of the dilet-tante, who turns to a section labeled Ásatrú in a book on Wicca and is offended that I haven't corrected erroneous Wiccan beliefs regarding Ásatrú that you and I know just don't exist beyond the bottom of the Wiccan barrel. Such barrel-bottomers are no more likely to read my works than they are to do research themselves and catering to them is just not my *modus operandi*.

With that caveat in place, let me weigh in on a few intra-Ásatrú terminology debates. For the purpose of this work, I will refer to Ásatrú as belonging to the general set of religions labeled Pagan. These religions have four basic qualities, and it should be noted that this is an imperfect operational definition, constantly in flux, but is nonetheless the definition in use for this work.

The Author's Semi-Arbitrary Definition of "Pagan" Religions:
  1. They represent new, reconstructed or resurrected religions developed within the past 500 years, including ancient religions that were discontinuously practiced, reappearing within that completely arbitrary time frame.
  2. They are based, even tangentially, on European indigenous beliefs.
  3. A proportion of the members of that faith self-describe themselves as Pagan at this point in time, or have historically[15] described themselves as "Pagan."
  4. The faith developed in Europe or in a European community.

That being said, while *I* define Ásatrú as part of the set of religions labeled Paganism, I will use the preferred terms Heathen and Heathenry when referring collectively to Ásatrú and Ásatrúesque Paganism, in part because that is the preferred terminology, and in part because some Ásatrúar are quite insistent that they are not Pagan. As I do not use the term here in the spirit of membership in the modern Pagan community but instead in the more general comparative usage, I hope the distinction is forgiven by those who would object. I further place Ásatrú in the set of religions generally classed as reconstructionist, and I find objections to the terms Nordic or Germanic Recon-

---

[15] By historically, I mean in the past, for a specific reason and easily defined lack of time. In the case of Ásatrú, many Ásatrúar identified as Pagan in the early days of Modern Paganism, but adopted the term Heathen as the Modern Pagan community's goals and points of view began to diverge from their own.

structionism for the general class of reconstructionist religions that include Ásatrú and Ásatrúesque Paganism as exceedingly silly, as few Ásatrú will disagree that their faith is a reconstruction of a historic faith or a resurrection of a discontinuous one. This discussion of religion in such broad terms has little to do with the actual practitioners and what they call themselves, and I hope that my readers can see the value in broad definitions used for comparative theology.

Objections to the terms faith, path and religion and suggested replacements with "way of life" and the like are similarly rejected, as they have been from all parties of all faiths who have made this suggestion. I am aware that the current fashion is to say one has spirituality, not a faith or religion, but until this fashion provides a description of religion that distinguishes it from spirituality on the basis of more than one's relationship with one's former religion, I have no desire to follow it. Faith, Path and Religion are used almost interchangeably within this work. They have subtle contextual differences, but do not represent a degree of dedication or validity, nor do they represent one type of religion over the other. Like the term mythology, I am fully willing to use the terms faith, path and religion on all religions, and do not reserve them for religions I believe in or reject.

This linguistic discussion and extensive operational definition clarification should not be construed as a difficulty on the part of the Ásatrúar who participated in the creation of this section. Indeed, the annoying vocal minority was not indulged and in addition was given the treatment it deserved. Instead, it was the well-spoken, generally cordial individuals who participated. That being said, this section does indeed represent information pertaining to the whole of this work and the previous one. I am simply too annoyed at linguistic quibbling to indulge in it. I have stated the terms I am using and why I am using them, and I hope that any reasonable discussions of what I state within this work hinge on the actual content, not which words a critic prefers.

This practice, of establishing your operational definitions before you use them, then restating them when you reach a point where you feel a person who has skipped that earlier section is likely to begin, is a time-honored and efficient technique. To those for whom this entire section has been repetitive, I apologize profoundly. That I needed to spend so long discussing the terms I used and, indeed, justifying the very existence of this section, may bespeak a problem, but it is not mine, and I hope that by being excruciatingly clear I have managed to steer around it.

What is Ásatrú?

Ásatrú, as discussed previously, falls under the broad category of reconstructionism, which is defined as a set of religions which attempt to reconstruct an actual religion of the past. There are reconstructionist movements throughout the world, including reconstruction of earlier forms of Christianity and Judaism. Obviously Wicca, as a modern religion, is not a reconstruction of any culture, but since it is based on beliefs regarding indigenous Europeans, it is not uncommon for Wiccans and reconstructionists to find themselves butting heads over a critical issue.

As I have stated in the past, it is important when looking at religions that developed amongst a people to honor and understand the cultural context in which those religions evolved. Transmitted religions, like Christianity, are those that start in one place amongst one people and are transmitted, via the spread of those people (or in this case, the transmission of the religion to Romans and the spread of those Romans, who are generally not considered the original culture of Christianity[16].) Those non-transmitted indigenous religions, which have sometimes been called "native religions," are intrinsically linked with a specific culture—inseparably so—and the study of the religion involves the study of its context.

For this reason, any halfway decent overview of Ásatrú will include a discussion of several terms that are native to the cultures Ásatrú evolved within, but are not necessarily always religious in their usage. I have the distinction of knowing several scholars of language who have often encountered the phenomena of finding a student who cannot see the meanings of a term beyond the religious use as they study language, so I will use my last caveat in this much-disclaimed section to state that no term defined within here is defined with the accuracy of a scholar. The usages I give are contextual, and common. I make no claim

---

[16] In my personal opinion, Christianity is wholly Roman, thanks to good old Paul, but that's a topic for another book.

of scholastic merit in any language, and have the distinction of never having formally studied any of the native languages of Ásatrú, so do not take my word as the definitive say on any of this. You will note that I have provided an extensive collection of recommended reading for those beyond the overview level, but I do not feel much more than an overview is required in a book for Wiccans, even ones studying Ásatrú with comparative theology in mind.

That being said, we can discuss what Ásatrú is. It is a religion in the truest sense of the word, a religion that exists with all of its cultural ties intact, without clear distinctions between one's identity as part of a culture and one's identity as part of a religion. This is typical of indigenous beliefs, even those that have been reconstructed or resurrected. While many Ásatrúar will paint this as a unique feature of their religion, (which, I have stated, they may choose not to term a "religion") it is actually a common feature when you look at religions in terms of numbers of religions instead of numbers of followers. It is really only Christianity that divorces culture from religion, a necessity when you wish to base the largest segment of your church in the capital city of the empire that killed your chief demigod.

It is important to have this understanding of the linkage between religion and culture when studying Ásatrú, perhaps more so than any other reconstructionist or indigenous faith. This is because Ásatrú is sometimes considered a reactionary movement to the destruction of its cultures by Abrahamic outsiders and a result of the Abrahamic mythos' rigid Middle Eastern core ideology, which obviously grows less relevant the further one goes from the Middle East. This makes it similar in many ways to the Celtic Reconstructionism we discussed in Topic Four.

Those similarities often include distrust for Wiccans — probably as a result of the inane behavior of a vocal minority that many outside the Wiccan community would be surprised to find out insult Wiccans even more than they insult non-Wiccans. Ásatrú, like core Wicca, is profoundly and literally polytheistic; but as a religion invested in a specific set of cultures it does not recognize gods outside of a Germanic or Norse Pantheon. This is not always exclusive Pantheonic polytheism, the belief that the whole of the gods that exist are those within the pantheon. More often, this is simply a lack of concern regarding the reality or deeds of gods outside the pantheon. When one has a set of gods who are functioning quite well in that capacity, the gods of other pantheons are usually unimportant.

It is perhaps because of this refined focus that Ásatrú often acknowledges the similarities between gods within the large Indo-European language group without making claims about one god coming from another. This is a common distinction in liberal polytheists, who tend to see similarities between pantheons as close to the similarities we see between families or a trend within the gods and their relationships rather than as some sort of theogenic methodology.

Like the Romans and their Romantic languages and cultures, which many of us are familiar with, the Germanic language group and related cultures were widespread and interrelated. Two results of this simple fact come to mind immediately. First, you're reading what is essentially an Anglo-Saxon polyglot[17], and second, Ásatrú is not a single form of Reconstructionism but a number of forms with much in common.

Ásatrú[18] is a Norse term meaning a faith or belief in gods. These gods, the Æsir[19], are the indigenous gods of the peoples

[17] The term polyglot is actually a good example. It comes from the Greek word(s) *polyglotta*, most literally many tongues. The phrase "you're reading what is essentially an Anglo-Saxon polyglot" contains, in order, Middle English (Germanic) "you are reading what is" Middle English from French: "essentially" Old English: "an" New Latin: "Anglo" Middle English from German, through Latin: "Saxon" and, of course, Greek. This is a good example of the Germanic foundation of our English language, as about 60% of the sentence is from Old German via Middle English, including most of the vital vocabulary, and the other 40% comes from a seemingly random collection of neighbors, invaders and tourists.

[18] According to http://www.irminsul.org/arc/022.html, the terms *Vor tru, "our faith," or Forn Sed, "ancient customs/ways"* are also used, but Ásatrú seems to be the more common term, and is used within for that reason. Based on what I have seen, those who would use the alternate terms would recognize the term Ásatrú, but not necessarily the other way around. Here I use Ásatrú as the proper noun for the faith, and throughout the section I will also use Ásatrú to mean what common English would probably call Ásatrú-ism or Ásatrú-ity, this is, again, a common convention, and should not worry my readers too much. We see it regularly with other faiths that end in vowels, including Wicca and Baha'I, where the vowel followed by –ism or –ity is just too annoying.

[19] Æsir will be used here to speak of both the male deities and the *Asyniur*, the female deities, this is not an uncommon convention that is inherently flawed, but convenient, and so I ask the forgiveness and understanding of those offended by it. I am also, intentionally, leaving out the Vanr (Vanir) in what I hope is the

who spoke Germanic languages. Most of us are familiar with some of their Norse forms, thanks to the comparative mythology we all absorb as children, where "comparative" means Greek and a handful of other gods from dozens of other cultures, taught as counterparts to the Greek gods. This is a frighteningly oversimplified view of the big picture, indicative, I believe, of the suspicion in our language that things our ancestors actually worshipped weren't nearly as interesting as the exotic or foreign gods of the Mediterranean (a belief I think opened the doors for mass extinction and repression of our indigenous religions, but that's another book!).

This leads to the inevitable question of which believers in the Æsir constitute Ásatrú. In general, there are four branches in Ásatrú's family tree. In *Four Bedposts of Ásatrú,* by Dirk Mahling of Medoburg Kindred, these four branches are described as "a house with four rooms (Scandic, Gothic, Anglo-Saxon and Southern)." I am uncomfortable with the common definition, like that of other minority faiths, that the Ásatrú know others when they see them, but it is the general opinion of most Ása-trúar that I have spoken to that, beyond general belief in the Æsir and a set of practices, the term Ásatrú, coined in the 19th century by scholars of the Norse epics, is really fairly loose. That being said, most Ásatrú agree on what they are not, so it is not a word that is nonsensical when used without disclaimers, as are Pagan or Witch.

What do the Ásatrúar believe?

The aforementioned *Four Bedposts of Ásatrú,* while not a universal Ásatrú writing, holds a good example of the central tenets of Ásatrú. As should be expected, this writing contains a lot of negative definitions — definitions that explain what Ásatrú is not, rather than what Ásatrú is. While this makes a good overview, it is not altogether helpful when people ask what Ásatrú is, so I chose this document because of the presence of positive definitions, as opposed to the lack of negative ones. While negative definitions are annoying from a scholastic point of view, they are at the root of most Indo-European cultures, where defining one-

spirit of inclusiveness. In my research, I noted the Æsir were nearly universal, while the Vanir were not.

self against The Stranger is commonplace[20], so they should not be misjudged as ethnocentrism or aggression.

Four Bedposts of Ásatrú *by Dirk Mahling of Medoburg Kindred*[21] (Used with Permission)

1. *Ásatrú is the dedication to (and only to) the Æsir and Vanir: Wotan, Donar, Woldur, Frolng, and friends. These gods are not a jealous lot, but Ganesh is by no stretch of imagination an Æsir. The nature of these gods (entity, archetype, etc.) is an ongoing discussion.*

2. *Ásatrú is the blot and sumbel on the greatest holydays (Yul, Ostara, Midsummer) to honor the Æsir and Vanir, heroes and ancestors. Other holidays exist (Walpurgis, Lammas, Harvest, Einherjar).*

3. *Ásatrú is the daily life of courage based on the thews of our ancestors - i.e., to take responsibility for our own deeds, to act true and honest, to be self-reliant and step in for freedom. Such a life creates good orlog. Ásatrú is DOING - not thinking and talking.*

4. *Ásatrú is a revitalized religion. A synthesis of literary/mythological sources of all Germanic folk (and the mix-ins from their Germanicized neighbors), contributions from scientific research (linguistics, history, anthropology, archeology, etc.) and deep personal insights. Ásatrú is a house with 4 rooms (Scandic, Gothic, Anglo-Saxon and southern). Regardless of our room, the street-address must be right.*

In addition we have quite a bit of gravy: runes, seidh, galdor, spae, lower mythology, holy steads, utisetta, tradition, family, tools, symbols, music, art, education, etc.

---

[20] On a tangential note, my recent hobby has been making my way **very** slowly through an online polyglot Bible, going through the *Koine* bible and comparing it to the Latin Vulgate and the King James (non-standardized.) One of the things that I have noticed in these is the ratcheting up of the comparison with The Stranger (capitalized because he is a sort of cultural archetype.) This is even stronger when you read the Hebrew Bible, where the majority of Non-Jews are generally just ignored save when they are a source of conflict. When compared to the schizoid Greek view in classical literature-the cultural need for treating the stranger properly and the absolute xenophobia for non-Greeks, I perceive a pattern that I feel radiates out from the Mediterranean.

[21] As presented at http://www.reeves-hall.org/bedposts.htm and http://www.geocities.com/heimdalls_lur/bedposts.html

Yet if you can't accept the four main points, you will be having trouble with Ásatrú.

In my opinion, these four points are fairly self-explanatory, but in many ways are problematic. It is difficult to gauge a religion based on the facts that it basically involves a specific set of gods; a specific set of holy days; doing, not thinking or talking; or the fact that it is, as Mahling puts it, revitalized. These definitions share many of the same problems as those I used in the previous sections on Ásatrú, they are (of necessity) vague. I am not, however, in the scholastic position to defend or critique them, and prefer to leave you with them as-is, sans further comment on my part.

Why a Section on Ásatrú in a Book for Wiccans?

There are a number of reasons why it is important for Wiccans to be aware of Ásatrú. Some of these have been discussed already, such as the belief of many Ásatrúar that Wiccans think their gods are part of a great one God or mere archetypes. Others are more complicated, and it to those things that I hope to speak in this section.

Wiccans are generally aware of perceived threats to Wicca or problems with Wiccans possessed by those outside the Pagan community. Since many are solitary practitioners, it is not unusual that they are utterly unaware of problems within the community and that there is strife between groups. One of the important facets I perceive in studying "advanced Wicca" is knowledge of the communities you are a part of — their borders, limits and problems — and the Ásatrú-Wiccan tension is one such problem.

It is part of a larger problem of strife between Wiccans and Reconstructionists, or more accurately, a problem with a specific minority of Wiccans and everyone else. This specific minority is well-known to most of the other Wiccans out there. They are, in general, spiritual privateers, co-opting the rituals, spaces and places of other people without regard for the damage they leave in their wake. Since they claim to be speaking for all Wiccans (and often all Pagans), it is not a surprise that some take them seriously.

For many years, the general Wiccan reaction to those who objected to such things was that we should live and let live, the idea being that these privateers were not really hurting anyone and that it was more important to stand with our Wiccan brothers and sisters against the perceived attacks of an outside community than to defend parts of our inner community from attacks from within. I have some small pride in saying that I, personally, built a reputation amongst such live-and-let-livers as a snob, a meanie and an egghead upon the foundation that harming other members of our community was something I felt personally reprehensible and something which I felt obligated to speak out against. They are beliefs that I hold to this day.

This strife exists on a number of levels, which I will attempt to illustrate, but I beg forgiveness for any biases that may creep into my illustrations in advance. Some of this strife has personally affected my life, and as a result, some of my own nerves are raw regarding it. Since this section is designed to make readers aware of a problem they may've managed to miss, not to make them take sides, I hope to remain objective in my imperfect manner.

Leaving behind the obnoxious minority, the main cause of this problem is the identification of the Pagan community itself. In general, the Pagan community defines itself by fairly subjective lines; we throw out the word Pagan and see who rushes up to claim the word. When we first encounter types that we don't like to see under our personal umbrella, we refine our concept of Pagan, often attempting to remove those unwanted elements. As we refine these statements of "paganism," we often exclude people we've no business excluding, and that is often the beginning of the strife.

Let me break off on a tangent for a moment to say that this is, of course, in the imaginary world where every group is being judged fairly. I have no intention of speaking to the ignorant people who disrupt the community by making unwarranted claims about other people's gods, practices, cultures or languages. Such people disrupt the community by virtue of their immense ignorance. We will collectively imagine, for this section, that such people do not exist and that the narrowing of the definition of the Pagan community is done only along lines that are based in reality, even if shaky reality.

One of those lines is often The Wiccan Rede, or more often a poor interpretation of it. Pagan communities will often state that their community is made up of "those who follow 'harm none' or a similar belief." The problem here, other than the obvious one, is that this excludes all faith-groups for whom a prohibition against harm is not a central tent of their faith. Taken to the extreme, this includes Wiccans, but taken as it often is—as the belief that groups that are Pagan have an equivalent of The Rede—very few religions have such equivalents...Pagan becomes "Wiccan only.

We do see prohibitions of harm, reasonable or unreasonable, in forms of Paganism that have sprung from Wicca, but Ásatrú and many other Pagan and Heathen religions evolved separately from Wicca, and as a result they do not have easily enumerated sets of beliefs that fit easily on a Wiccan framework. To therefore attempt to define them by the Wiccan Rede, Law of Return or any other predominantly Wiccan teaching is to do them a disservice, and exclude them unfairly.

Similarly, many people attempt to define Paganism by their social or political views of choice, or by the practice of certain metaphysical rites and techniques. Environmentalism, Libertarianism, Magic and Astrology are embraced by many Pagans, but not all Pagans. To associate membership in a Pagan community with any of these things, or to claim words like Earth-Based or Green as equivalent to Pagan systematically pushes many Pagans who have used the words for years out of your definition.

This is exacerbated by the fact that many of the heads of Pagan organizations who do such things are Wiccan or (much more often) Wiccanesque Pagans, which has led to a general sensation of Wiccans as The Borg of Paganism, trying to fit all these people who got along fairly well when their communities were small into their little boxes by assimilation rather than affiliation. Such ideas are understandable but misguided, for the Pagan community has always been highly dynamic and fluid.

It becomes a totally fair question to ask when one asks if Paganism means anything at all. While this is a reasonable question, it is not a fair one for answering *at this time*. With that in mind, however, it may not surprise you that the problems some Ásatrúar have with the Pagan community is not being excluded from it, but being included in it without consultation. People have written books and manifestos in which Ásatrúar were called Wiccans or offshoots of Wicca when they aren't, something we should all know by now.

In general, all the strife can be characterized as wounded pride in the fact that would-be Pagan leaders will speak for people they have no business speaking for, punctuated by actual cases of discrimination, insensitivity and just genuine obnoxiousness. Many Wiccans, for example, will often make themselves heard for no apparent reason, as if the fact that a thing exists warrants the world's attention to Wiccan beliefs regarding it. It would be a lie to say no Wiccan ever went to the papers to speak for all Wiccans, and many go beyond it and say, quite without shame, that they speak for Wiccans and all other followers of the "old" gods. This and other embarrassing tendencies have caused a deep wound that is in need of treatment in the Pagan community, a wound that every Wiccan should be aware of. In the end, it is my belief that the community will divide and only come back together if threatened by a common enemy. The exchanges lost with this divide sadden me, but are probably for the best.

Having laid out some of the dynamics of the community of which we Wiccans and the Ásatrúar are both currently members, perhaps even founding members, I hope that I have illustrated the reasons why this section was needed, even if not explicitly. For those for whom explicitness is required, however, I shall end this chapter section with a firm answer:

This section exists because Wiccans, as a majority within the Pagan community, are required to hold that position with honor and decency, as our faith dictates. To this end, we must be aware of the non-Wiccan members of the community, both of their existence and of their faith, and in seeking to live in a way that does minimal harm, stay out of their way. We must not exclude them from — or include them in — our community without their input and we can definitely, definitely, not claim to speak on their behalf. If we tell no lies about them and make no claims about them, they will likely do the same for us. We let them speak for themselves and we speak for ourselves. We must be aware of the existence of the tensions, and their sources, without adding to them.

While we do not need to be scholars of these other faiths, we should have enough knowledge of them to filter the data we receive reasonably and carefully. For example, a Wiccan Priest encountering a young student with an interest in the Æsir should be ready and prepared to point out to that student that perhaps Ásatrú would be a better choice than Wicca. He can not do that if he does not know it exists, nor that these gods are theirs.

Above all else, we must be aware that Ásatrú and many other religions are not types of Wicca or offshoots of Wicca, nor do they share our goals. In the end, this lack of shared goals may cause the communities to may grow apart, but better that should be an amicable parting than a war. At this time, while we are not as persecuted as some would claim, there are dangers we mutually share, and until those dangers have gone, we may come together as members of a community with that in common, if nothing else.

The obligatory section on Racism, Ethnocentricity and Indigenous Religions

It is with a tangible sensation of annoyance that I begin this section. Like the simple fact that there is tension between Ásatrúar and Wiccans in the community, the fact that there are issues regarding the stereotype of all Ásatrú as racists is something that you can become aware of with very little effort. That so many Wiccans are unaware this issue exists just boggles my mind, and it is to that end I've composed this section and labeled it "obligatory." For those for whom this is old news, again, forgive me.

Ancestral religions are often seen as racist. Many of them are focused on the idea that it is blood that conveys the power. For example, in the FMT I mentioned in 333, they genuinely believe that they are descended from a direct line of power and that that decent conveys the power. For reasons I do not fully comprehend, some people see this as very, very unfair. To the family, however, it is as if they are carriers of a rare gene, and that that gene conveys the power of their line.

When it is things like immunity to certain medical conditions, hair color, family lands or certain tendencies that you pass on to your children it is generally not considered an issue, but say that you are handing them an ability that other people don't have and you become a racist to many people. I *can't* explain such beliefs because I do not understand them myself. However they exist, and this larger idea is often a source of tension with Ásatrúar.

The example I gave is actually much more extreme than the situation in Ásatrú, but my incomprehension at the perceived problem with such situations flavors my reactions, so again, try to bear with me. As I have mentioned, Ásatrú is inextricably linked with its core cultures, and the result of this is that membership in the culture is generally perceived as a prerequisite for participation in the religion. They don't really exist separately, so that's an oversimplification, but a reasonable one.

It is this distinction—membership in the culture—that most Ásatrúar make when excluding people from their ranks. What membership in the culture *is* varies from group to group. For most, it is generally a sincere desire to follow the Æsir in a way that does not clash with the historic ways to do so. For a minority, membership in the culture is defined as having some sort of easily definable characteristic—speaking the language proficiently, for example. For the slimmest of minorities, that characteristic is white skin or a traceable Germanic lineage. The flaws in the first of these will be discussed briefly, but let me state that the second of these I understand when the group is focused upon a specific ancestor.

A friend of mine is a member of a group descended from one Welshman, and they have an association of blood relationships. His group is all different colors, but related to their progenitor by blood. I can understand the desire of some Heathen groups to resurrect and strengthen the concept of strong bonds in direct family, a concept that modern culture often denies. This is especially good among those groups who define themselves as a familial group within the culture and recognize that others exist within the culture who are not of those families. Familial organizations are a wonderful thing, and when they are associated with religious practice can be doubly so. It is not racist or wrong to say that only people related to you, by blood or even by recognized adoption and rites like marriage, are your family.

Racist groups, on the other hand, base their membership on perceived visual cues. I suspect that there could be an equitable way of doing this. An association of red headed stepchildren, for example, could determine that any red-headed stepchild was welcome in their membership, and they could work together towards goals that they, as red headed stepchildren, shared. (No doubt this would be the prevention of cruelty to red-headed stepchildren!) Racists, however, aren't really interested in skin color or visual cues. People of any ethnicity who are albino, for example, have pale skin and hair — and certainly an albino without white parents wouldn't be welcome in the KKK, because he would just "look white" not "be white."

The Ásatrúar have a two-fold problem with racism. On the one hand, their culture's religious relics, symbols and more have been co-opted by racists and other altogether not-nice individuals, so there will be those who assume that they are racist on that basis, the basis of their symbolism, a problem they share with members of Vedic religions wanting to use the swastika and those in Religio Romana who'd like to use the fasces. People who so assume may choose to discriminate against them on this basis or may assume that they share their racist views and seek to join with them on this basis. On the other hand, it's not a far leap, if not a totally logical one, from ethnic religion and pride to ethnocentrism and exclusion. That it is not a logical leap is not enough to stop people from doing it. Many humans are quite illogical.

This shouldn't be taken as claiming that Ásatrú doesn't have racists. There *are* racist groups that are Ásatrú-based, or perhaps better named Ásatrú-esque, groups that are often but not always called by the problematic moniker "Odinism." These groups sometimes have no theological basis for their racism and sometimes manipulate their theology to support their goals.

The idea that only blood relatives of the original people of the Æsir may participate in Ásatrú, which is a more reasonable statement by far than that only white people, who may not be any shade of Germanic in origin, may participate, is not a difficult one to grasp, but it has a major flaw. Few scholars deny that adoption and marriage practices occurred in Northern Europe, so the theologically sound point of view of the non-racist (and even the non-blood-based) Ásatrúar is that a person can be added to the culture, thus fulfilling the "membership in the culture" prerequisite.

Related to this, tangentially, is the fact that many Ásatrúar do have issues with multiple cultural affiliations. It is difficult for many of them to grasp syncreticism, the blending of Ásatrú with other religions, as a valid path. On a personal note, I think some level of syncreticism is valid whenever we deal with ancient peoples because ancient peoples dealt with other ancient peoples and it was inevitable that somewhere there were ancient families and individuals who hedged their bets and prayed both sides of the Pantheon. That being said, I personally disagree with blending the rites of one god with the rites of another and don't practice it in my own life. However, I do hold affiliations in more than one faith and do not consider the non-blended practice of two non-conflicting faiths to be bad.

For many Ásatrúar, however, in addition to the worship of the Æsir only in their rites, there is an assumption that those within the community only worship the Æsir, ever. This may or may not be a reasonable assumption on their parts, and it may or may not be a reasonable qualification for membership in the community. In this matter, I will remain silent. Those who seek a syncretic path should be aware of the problems, but it is not my place to condemn them for it.

Recommended Reading for Topic Seventeen:
Offline:

Penguin Classics has a selection of books important to Ásatrú, mostly related folklore. These highly accessible translations are often used by schools and colleges, and they generally use decent translators. That being said, my personal in-depth experience with these works is limited to one of them, The Agricola and Germania of Tacitus, a translation I found well readable.

Penguin Classics:

The Agricola and the Germania of Tacitus (Mattingly et al, translating)

Beowulf: A Prose Translation David Wright (Editor)

Beowulf, Michael Alexander (Editor)

Beowulf: A Verse Translation, Michael Alexander (Editor)

Egil's Saga Hermann Pálsson et al.

Eyrbyggja Saga Hermann Pálsson et al.

Hrafnkel's Saga and Other Stories trans. by Hermann Pálsson

King Harald's Saga (Snorri Sturluson, Magnus Magnusson)

Laxdaela Saga (Magnus Magnusson)

Njals Saga (Magnus Magnusson)

The Nibelungenlied translated by A.T. Hatto

Other Offline:

True Hearth: A Practical Guide to Traditional Householding. (Chisholm) (Runa-Raven Press)

The Complete Illustrated Guide to Runes. (Pennick) (I like all of his stuff, anyway.)

Nordic Gods and Heroes (Colum)

...as well as anything by Edred Thorsson

Online:

http://www.geocities.com/heimdalls_lur/wiccaasatru.html (The Pentagram and the Hammer, a well-distributed essay on Wicca and Ásatrú. I have some minor issues with the text, but it is good, and for those for whom a compare-and-contrast type essay is preferable to a survey-type essay, it is an excellent read. The flaw I see in such essays [like "Why Wicca is Not Celtic" and the defunct "Wicca and Hellenismos, a comparison"] is that they expect that the readers concur with both their definitions of the contrasting faith and with Wicca. I prefer, instead, to attempt to provide decent material on both and allow the reader to make their own comparisons and contrasts, which some will say outright is expecting too much of you.)

http://www.webcom.com/~lstead/IntroAsatru.html (a basic introduction)
http://www.thetroth.org/ourfaith/intro.html (a Basic "about")

http://www.irminsul.org/arc/011ht.html (A glossary of terms)

http://www.irminsul.org/arc/022.html (A FAQ)

http://members.iquest.net/~chaviland/whyasa.htm (another "about")

More Ásatrú Related Links (with links to more resources):
http://huginn.ealdriht.org/   (Heathen Search Engine)
http://www.thetroth.org/
http://www.irminsul.org/ (The Extensive Links section and Contact map here is why I generally send people looking for services similar to those of The Witches' Voice but with a Heathen Focus to this site.)

Discussion Questions for Topic Seventeen:

17.1. Why is it important for Wiccans to study other religions?

17.2. What does the author mean when she says that Druids, Ásatrúar and others are abused by the Pagan community?

17.3. What are the essential beliefs of Ásatrú?

17.4. What is the basis for Ásatrú?

17.5. What is the problem in the Pagan community that the author says Solitaries are often unaware of?

17.6. How important is it that Wiccans know the sources of strife toward them?

17.7. Do you think the author approves of "Norse Wicca?" Do you? Why or why not?

17.8. What is the difference between a racist group and a heritage based(blood-based) group?

17.9. Is the society for the prevention of cruelty to red-headed stepchildren, which only allows red headed stepchildren to join, racist?

17.10. According to the author, how do Ásatrúar generally perceive syncreticism?

Topic Eighteen: The Druids

Ancient Druidry[22]: What do we know?

Druidry is a sticky subject. While there is lots of evidence for the existence of Druids amongst the ancient Celts, their actual practices are poorly documented. This is not to say that there is no information, a common claim that has led to an atmosphere that anything can pawned off onto the public as Druidry. Indeed, there is a great wealth of information — archaeological sites, contemporary histories and even surviving folk practices and stories that have been documented for several centuries. What we lack, however, is a firsthand account of ancient practice... a book, for example, written by a Druid about his life. Similarly, we lack any biographies or survey works on Druidry from non-interested third parties that were contemporaries with them. Such works would be incredibly helpful, but they just don't exist.

We have instead a huge collection of circumstantial and biased information, and as any good lawyer, or indeed any fan of courtroom dramas, can tell you, this *can* be enough information to make a case for the truth. It just requires a bit more work than we would like to do, generally. The problem, as always, is that some people have taken this circumstantial and biased information and used the bits and pieces that justify their particular beliefs and extrapolated that they, therefore, are practicing the ancient religion of the druids.

This is normally where I would use an outrageous example, probably with someone named Joe or Fred, to explain how they do this and why it is silly. I am refraining at this point only because we know how Joe and Fred did it — they got something into their head, picked up a crappy book on Druidry or went to a poorly written website and skimmed until they found something that supported what was in their head, whereupon they labeled the practices they made up before picking up a single book or going to a single website "Druidry." I refrain from giving the silly example because by now, even if you haven't read 333,

---

[22] There is some debate over whether the term Druidry or Druidism is more appropriate. I use Druidry out of personal preference.

you're aware of this behavior and that it is wrong, and that I object to it on several levels.

So, that aside, what do we know about Ancient Druidry?

In my opinion, the definitive book on Druidry, which I consulted repeatedly for this section, is Peter Beresford Ellis' 1994 work *The Druids*, and it is to that work I commend any readers who wish to know more details than the few scarce ones given here. The problem with any format like this one is that you get only the briefest of introductions in the spirit of comparison and knowledge and that many of these topics (especially 17-20 in this work) really deserve to be studied in extreme detail. This makes people like me, who want to fill my head and the heads of others with as much as possible, exceedingly annoyed, because if you were here in my office, I'd thrust the book at you, say see you in a few hours and be done with it.

Since I can't do that, nor force you to travel to the bookstore, real or virtual, and hold you down until you purchase it, I'm limited to sort of condensing and paraphrasing the wonderful materials Ellis and a handful of others have birthed. The next few paragraphs consist of a condensed and paraphrased summary from the Recommended Reading at the end of this topic, but I strongly suggest going to that reading, even more so than I suggest it with other topics.

The Druids were a subgroup of the Celts, most likely an upper caste. As members of this upper caste, they received more education than the average person, and it seems they passed this education and caste status down to their children. In Celtic mythology, many heroes are described as the children of Druids, and certainly there were female Druids, so it was likely a status held by families. It is the contention of many modern day Celtic Reconstructionists that "Druid" was a title, similar to Rabbi in the Abrahamic religions. This is not altogether unlikely, but the *Druidae* and *Dryades* written of by the Greeks seemed to encompass more of a class of people from which than those in leadership are chosen than anything else.

While the Greeks called female Druids *Dryades*, there is little indication that these dryads were the same as the mythological ones. Certainly there is no evidence of the Celts calling female Druids "dryads," despite the attempts of some fringe Pagans to claim otherwise. The similarity between dryad and Druid are generally believed to be a result of having two words that are related to the same Proto-Indo-European root, probably the word for oak. There is a strong possibility that the second half of the word is the "vid" root word (video, for example) which pertains to seeing. Thus those that claim that Druid (or dryad) means "Oak seers" are not on altogether shaky etymological ground, but the importance of this is questionable. Indeed, the rowan is can be seen as the most important tree to the Druids within folklore, and other trees play an important part in what we know of their religion.

Another common claim regarding the druids was that they were involved in human sacrifice. If any of the Celts practiced human sacrifice, something that Julius Caesar claimed, it was a very rare occurrence. While some claim they killed once a year based on finds of a very few bodies in peat bogs that some think appear to have been ritually slain, it didn't happen nearly as often as that — and based on the condition of the bodies and the survival of dying king stories in Celtic Lore, it may've been something that happened only in times of the greatest strife and done willingly. More likely those few things that point to sacrifices represent what we might term legitimate executions, or maybe even small fringe cults at the edge of society.

That being said, those who paint Caesar's writings of human sacrifice as baseless propaganda seem to be pretty unaware of the Roman lack of squeamishness in killing criminals, enemy warriors and undesirables. It is unlikely Caesar would've made something up completely out of whole cloth with the desire to enrage people against an enemy and done it half-way. More likely, the general was relying on biased information from his sources. If he wanted to get Rome up in arms, he probably would've talked about mass cannibalism and other things that prominent in Roman literature used to describe enemies.

What the Druids certainly had was knowledge of herbalism, astronomy, metaphysics, leadership skills and more. There is no evidence they had impossible to replicate technologies, but plenty of evidence that they were, perhaps, the most advanced physicians of their time, with the discovery of trepanated skulls just part of that evidence. Despite their goals as lore-keepers, their rituals and their skills, Ellis contends that Druidry was not a profession, but a social caste, an educated elite. Based on the

evidence he presents and my own study of cultures contemporary with the Druids, I'm inclined to agree, and I find myself
with those amongst the Celtic Reconstructionists who limit their
use of the term Druid to indicate those few within the CR community who fit the description of "educated elite."

I recognize as well two other groups of Druids, who I refer
to by the terms "Fraternal Druids" and "Modern Druids," and I
accept these terms only because I genuinely feel they have the
power of time, even if only a few generations, behind them. It is
because of these two groups that there is broad interest in
Druidry, and they are worthy of discussion for that reason, even
if their connection to a Druidic past is less genuine then that of
the Celtic Reconstructionists. That being said, there is evidence
to support the theory that the lines between classes were blur-
ring before the Romans or Christians ever influenced the Druids,
which is why many Celtic Reconstructionists don't use the title
Druid at all. Had they never met an outside influence it is still
likely there would be no contemporary Celtic Druids.

I mention this because within the Celtic Reconstruction and
Preservation communities I deal with regularly as an interested
outsider, the use of the term Druid by non-CR groups and individuals is a strong issue for some, and a non-issue for others. As
with most things, it seems, the definition of what really consti-
tutes a Druid is a very dynamic one, full of personal prejudices.
For me, the only "real" Modern Druids are those descended
from the fraternal societies and those given the title by Celtic
Reconstructionists. Since that probably covers 99% of the Druids
in the Modern World, it's not exactly a radical distinction.

A Brief Note about Fraternal Druidic Societies

I mentioned in the last section that in my study of Druidry
and Celtic religion, I personally accept only two definitions of
the label Druid. The first of these two uses is that of the term
Druid by Celts to identify members of an educated caste within
their ranks, either in the past or in Reconstructionist communities. The second use is that of the term to indicate membership in
a fraternal druidic society, including the Modern Druid societies
descended (even tangentially) from them.

Let it not be said that I am fully comfortable with this second
usage. In explaining it in the past, I have stressed two facts that
allow me to make this distinction. The first is that the body of

time is behind the use of the term in this way, with the 1781 creation of The Ancient Order of the Druids trumping the Celtic Reconstructionist movement by nearly two centuries. The second is that, frankly, fraternal organizations often have silly names, and I do not consider membership in the Druid Fraternities to make one a "Druid" in the classical sense any more than I consider membership in the Elks to make one a large herbivore. Similarly, many of my Masonic friends cannot carve a stone, and I have never seen a Lion make an appearance at a Lions club. Clearly to hold *other* fraternal organizations to the same standard many hold the Druidic Fraternal associations is unfair, but, that being said, it should be stated that no fraternal associations are out there doling out the terms rabbi or priest to their membership, and for those for whom the title Druid holds similar meanings the distinction is not so easy.

If you have learned anything from my section on Ásatrú, and the sections on the Celts and others, let it be the simple fact that it is nearly impossible to speak about anything poorly written of without creating definitions, definitions that are often inherently flawed. For this reason I attempt to state the source of my definitions and my reasoning up front, so that my terms and phrases can be used or discarded as the reader sees fit. Where possible, I use the terminology of people whose work I respect, unless I find the definitions unworkable, as I do with Neopagan, for example. It is in that spirit that I consider only these two classes of Druids to be Druids, not in the spirit of exclusion, and I think you'll find that it's a broader definition than it might seem at first.

That being said, since no Druids in the classical sense exist today outside of potential Reconstructionist groups that could re-adopt the term for their educated elite, we'll stick to the Druids of the past 250 years or so. Early fraternal associations claiming the term Druid were primarily invested in the preservation of ancient languages, cultures and folkways, which is not surprisingly a huge focus of the Reconstructionist movements today; however, these groups were highly invested in erroneous ideas about the ancient Druids, beliefs that are no longer considered likely. These early Druids used a diverse collection of source materials, ranging from archaeology to pure fiction, and as later organizations built upon these earlier ones, much of this false material of the past was transported to the present with the weight of time upon it to lend it some credibility, resulting in the issues discussed in Topic Four regarding the Celts.

That being said, much of the mythology regarding the Druids and the Celts that these early revivalists were using had no bearing whatsoever on their rites and beliefs, as their rites were not those of a religion or a religious people at all. Contrary to the teachings of a few, the members of these groups were Christians, often with a heavy dose of nationalism, and not followers of any form of Paganism, Modern, Ancient or other. Thus those bizarre claims that such notables as Winston Churchill were Pagan on the basis of relationship with these fraternal organizations are just silly, as the Druids of those organizations had a lot more in common with Elks, Masons and Oddfellows than with Wiccans, Witches and Modern Druids.

There is, to my knowledge, no work which treats the seventeenth and eighteenth century druids with the thoroughness and lack of bias we see in Ellis' work regarding the classical ones, and while I am unimpressed with recent studies of Modern Druidry, at least those works exist. For the person attempting to synopsize this middle Druidry, this lack of quality source material is annoying, and I hope my own readers will forgive my brevity. A better person than I is needed to fill this gap.

Modern Druidry: None of the Above?

I grew up with Druids all around me. Friends of my family were practicing Druids, and one of the most active Druid Groves in the country practiced 15 minutes from my house. When I founded a local Pagan alliance, those Druids were some of the first folk I was put in contact with, and years before, when I first began actively researching Paganism as a possible life direction, the local Druid grove and ADF were front runners in the race. Had I not found Silver Chalice, which would later become UEW, this might be Druidry 334, not Wicca 334, and this might be a topic on Wicca in a book on Druidry, not vice versa.

While my choice is not something I regret, a dear friend, clanswoman and Celtic Reconstructionist insists that I am biased as a result of these positive encounters. While I think I am capable of writing objectively on the subject, she insists that I have an overly positive view of Modern Druids, and that this will inevitably creep into anything I write about them. I mention this, again, in the spirit of openness, and leave my bias or lack thereof for you to judge.

In general, the majority of people I have encountered who have been parts of a Druidic society belong to either ADF and groups that have sprung from it (or in imitation of it), or OBOD and groups that have sprung from it (or in imitation of it). I do not, from a personal point of view, consider independent people who pick up the term Druid to be using it accurately, because the two uses of the term I personally recognize both involve a social recognition — one, a membership in an educated elite of a specific people, the other, membership in an organization. To be alone and using the term seems very far from the concept of either modern or ancient groups, and I am uncomfortable with using any term for no definite reason. Perhaps those using it to mean Seers of Oaks and the like exist, and I could understand a reverse-engineering of beliefs from the etymology of the term, especially if it happened with a Jupiter-centric Romano-Celtic Reconstructionist[23]. However, I've never met a person using the term who was not a part of a group which could explain why they choose that term. That ability to explain "why" is a big deal to me, as far as legitimate usage is concerned.

In no particular order then, I will begin the discussion with the group with which I am more familiar, ADF. ADF, Ár nDraíocht Féin: A Druid Fellowship, takes its name from three Irish-Gaelic words which translate as "Our Own Druidism," and was founded in 1983 by Isaac Bonewits as what he describes as "a network of independent scholars interested in legitimate research about the ancient Druids and their Indo-European colleagues[24]." As he details on their website, it quickly grew into its

---

[23] Yes, there is such a thing. Strictly speaking, such people follow both a Roman and a Celtic Pantheon not in the sense of syncreticism, but in the sense of the "dual citizenship" of places like Gaul. I met my first Romano-Celtic Reconstructionist while trying to resolve the complex relationship between provincial and Roman gods in Cornwall with a friend of Cornish descent who held a similar interest in Roman archaeology and have since met several more.

[24] http://www.adf.org/about/qa.html (ADF website: Questions and Answers about ADF, Bonewits)

own sect of Paganism[25], with their own training programs, rituals and the like. Unlike many Druid groups, ADF is and has remained an independent entity with its own sets of standards, among which is a vital critique of revisionism and historical fantasy. As Bonewits says on their webpage, "The Goddesses and Gods do not need us to tell lies on their behalf, nor can we understand the ways of our Paleopagan predecessors by indulging in romantic fantasies, no matter how 'politically correct' or emotionally satisfying they might be.[26]"

If ADF's focus is upon creating a new Druidry of their own, OBOD[27], The Order of Bards, Ovates and Druids is upon creating (or preserving) the spirit of the fraternal Druidic organizations of the past, and finding the fine line between the atrocious scholarship of the past and the great works people are doing now. OBOD regularly gets a lot of (undeserved, in my opinion) bad press in the Pagan communities I have worked with, but I've never seen any evidence that genuine strife between OBOD, ADF and other groups exist, save for a few fringe organizations that seem to have problems with everyone else, anyway.

In general, OBOD tries to work within a fraternal framework similar to that they see in the centuries-old organizations they claim to be descended from. As a result of this, OBOD members share beliefs more as members of a community or culture, rather than as members of a shared religion. For this reason, OBOD has members of religions ranging from Christianity to Wicca, and everything in-between. In a way, this is similar to the way ancient Druids worked, although it could be argued, and has, that it is not unlikely that following ways other than traditional Celtic practices probably would've been bad news for one's continued membership in the elite caste of the Celts.

A third organization, the struggling British Druid Order[28], also warrants mention, but I don't have enough experience to

[25] Bonewits uses the term Neopagan exclusively, pretty much as exclusively as I use the term Pagan. My justification for this has been well-explained elsewhere, so assume that anywhere where I call ADF people "Pagans" he'd call them Neopagans.
[26] http://www.adf.org/about/vision.html (ADF Website: The Vision of ADF, Bonewits)
[27] http://www.druidry.org
[28] http://www.britishdruidorder.co.uk/home.htm

speak of them in anything but the most general of general terms. They have been more focused upon developing (or redeveloping) a native British Spirituality than upon the fraternal work of OBOD or the more generalized scholarship of ADF. They have more than a tangential relationship to OBOD, however, and while claiming they were related to OBOD is probably not something they'd refute, claiming anything beyond a tangential relationship is more than I desire to do. Regardless of the fact that BDO and similar groups bear a similarity to OBOD and ADF more, perhaps, by accident than by intent, I *still* think a study of Modern Druidry will find that all the other legitimate groups fit nicely into the two categories of ADF-like and OBOD-like.

The Celts versus the Druids

It was inevitable that when I began writing this section, I got a wee bit of fan mail that objected to my research on Druids, feeling I'd done enough on Celts in *Wicca 333*, and any more was overkill. I am open about what I am researching at any given time, and go into large communities, online and off, and ask questions. As I invite such mail, I appreciate the fears of those who expressed concern that this two-part "master class" in Wicca would become a huge rant against Celtic Wicca, and I hope that I have justified devoting two topics to what many see as one.

Unlike the previous section, this one is on Druids exclusively. As surprising as it may be to read, in my entire topic on the Celts, Druids aren't mentioned at all, a point which, taken with all the other data, led me to the conclusion that while I personally make a clear distinction between Druids and Celts, it is not so clear a distinction for other people. It may have been an oversight on my part to have not collected this brief topic into a single unit of Topic Four, and left the discussions of intellectual integrity and the like to another topic, but I find that at this stage of the work, with nearly eighteen topics behind us, it is not unlikely that you are able to flesh out the overview of the Druids I have provided in such a manner that those who need an deeper overview can find it, and those for whom this material is a boring continuation of Topic Four will find it blessedly brief.

That being said, the relationship between the Celts and the Druids is best defined with set theory: The Classical Druids are a set within the big set of Celts, whereas the Modern Druids comprise a set that includes members of the Celtic set, but not the whole of it—and "Celtic" is not a defining quality of their set. In other words, while the Ancient Druids were most assuredly Celts, the Modern Druids base their membership on shared beliefs, training and goals which transcend tribe, race, ethnicity and sometimes religion. In other words, a Classical Druid would've been a Celt, probably part of an educated social and economic class of the Celts, and it is likely s/he would've been trained in some sort of formal manner as a member of that social group. A modern Druid, however, is a Druid by virtue only of membership within a Druid organization, which usually requires some training but rarely, if ever, involves one social status or birth caste.

There is a general consensus that the Druids appeared to be dissolving as a social class before Roman influence began to affect Celtic life. For this reason, it is not an uncommon occurrence for Celtic Reconstructionist Organizations to avoid using the term at all. When I made the distinction between Wicca and Celtic Reconstructionism and Culture in 333, I did not use the term Druid for that very reason. As I have stated, it is not unlikely, given the evidence, that if no one had come and influenced the Celts, and they had continued to evolve without outside interference, their modern culture might still be Druid-free, as it is today (at least in the classical sense of the term Druid.)

So, therefore, we can make the main distinction quite easily: the Celts were, and still are, a group of people defined by shared culture and ethnicity, but the Druids were a specific subgroup of those people, slowly being phased out before the time when Celtic culture began to be heavily influenced by Roman culture and eventual Christianity. The distinction between them then becomes the distinction between members of a single ethnicity and culture and members of a clearly defined social caste and/or profession.

It is this distinction that allows Modern Druids to use their term quite accurately, while those attaching the adjective Celtic to every noun that cannot run fast enough to avoid them are in error. One is about membership in something difficult to define by anything more than the subjective concept of membership in an organization and the other is simply defined as membership in a culture, which, while difficult to define in and of itself, is something that members of that culture are quite capable of recognising.[29]

Similarities and Differences between Modern Druidry and Wicca

The reason I have devoted so much attention to Druidry is that it serves as a highly interesting foil to Wicca. Both began as a sort of reconstruction of a previous religion, and both were plagued with the simple fact that that ancient religion just wasn't what their founders thought it was. They remind me of two oak trees, sprouting from two acorns that fell side by side. At first, they were two separate saplings, growing from the same ground, but they were so close together that, after a while, they fused, but still show signs of being distinct entities, with parts of their root structure unique to each tree, and parts of it shared by the new conjoined entity.

There is similarity in the basis of the two religions that warrants mention, the result of shared roots in Theosophy and British spiritualism, and also a result of the relationship between Ross Nichols, founder of OBOD, and Gerald Gardner. There is a similarity in terminology, as well as the liturgical calendar, and it is not surprising that early in Wicca we see the Murray names for the eight high holy days replaced by the ones in use by OBOD, even if misspelled by the Wiccans. There is an early flow of ideas and concepts, which is attributed to multiple phenomena by different researchers, and rather than state my theories as to the cause, I will state merely my acknowledgement of the flow.

At the same time, there was a need for these two trees to grow independently, and during the period that the Expanded Tomas Timeline (ETT) calls "Middle Modern Wicca" the two

---

[29] In *Wicca 333*, I quite adamantly stated that I refuse to recognize any definition of Celt that includes me. In the time between writing this and writing that, I have been informed by no less than three people easily defined as Celts that I am in error, that as a person who studies (however poorly) a Celtic language, bears Celtic names in my family tree, and bears the sole non-Celtic name in my immediate family, amongst other things, I am, indeed, a Celt, and claims to the contrary are exactly that which I seek to avoid-using the definitions of non-members of a culture to define who is and is not a member. I affirm that I do consider myself a Celtic American, but if any Celts wish to claim otherwise of me, I guess I have to respect that or stand as a hypocrite.

grow in fairly different directions, Wicca focusing on magic and becoming associated with the self-improvement movement, and Druidry focusing more on ecology—both straying from a previous path of flawed Reconstructionism. This weaving, together then apart, would be brought back together again as the concept of a broader Pagan movement began to take hold. The exchange of ideas brought more ecology and Celtic imagery into Wicca and more self-improvement and Ceremonial Magic into Druidry, and is largely responsible for those within the Pagan movement who seek to define Paganism as the practice of magic or green spirituality. Essentially, those people are defining Paganism as a whole by these syncretic Wiccan-Druids who take on the additions as definitive qualities. That they often don't exist in the original core theologies is meaningless.

They move out again, in their patterns, as the myths of their respective "reconstructions" begin to unravel, and then come back as new research shows them to be siblings, and the pattern continues, *ad infinitum*, until we stand where we are now, with Modern Druidry heavily flavored by Modern Wicca and vice versa, and many proponents of both claiming no relationship at all whilst others claim no difference. This sort of religious incest is discomforting in a way, and a theoretician might suspect that eventually we shall see both become a sort of third path, a Druidic Wicca, or Wiccan Druidry, no doubt simply called Neopaganism.

Thus, in my no doubt controversial opinion, you cannot study differences between Wicca and Druidry save in those groups that have existed with little interface, and since I have not seen even one group whose claim to complete isolation has been proven valid, I believe Wicca and Druidry as practiced today are, essentially, the same entity with some vague cosmetic differences. This creates strife, of course, as people who joined either religion on the spaces in the patterns where they were well separated saw an outward focus on their differences, not their similarities, and those who came in when the union of the two faiths was in fashion don't see the need for separation.

This is not to say that Druid groups and Wiccan groups are exactly the same. The difference in focus, while primarily only a surface difference is nonetheless a completely valid one and the differences in liturgy are significant. The union is not in practice, although the similarities are there, but in culture and cosmology, where both ended up finding flaws in their original cosmology and mining the same third parties to fill in those flaws. Unlike Ásatrú and Reconstructionism, which are tangentially related to the Pagan cultural movement, Wicca and Druidry are inseparable parts of it. It is this similarity that leads to definitions of Pagan that are merely definitions of Wicca and Druidry, and a whole set of new problems associated with such flaws.

The error enters the equation simply because people see the similarities between the two faiths as accidental or the relationship between survivors of a common enemy, not deliberate transfer of data from one group of people to another. When that data transfer is recognized, it is easier to define the differences, by seeing where the commonalities came from and how the individual faiths reacted to that new information. It is for that reason I find the fused oak tree metaphor so very telling. It is, regardless of the root structure and history, only one plant, and if you chop half of the trunk the whole thing will die. Yet, even in this union, the newer branches are completely separate, and if one were to fall, it is unlikely they all would all perish, despite sharing some damage.

Recommended Reading for Topic Eighteen:

The Druids, Ellis, 1994.

http://www.unet.univie.ac.at/~a8700035/celtreli.html
 (Celtic Religion-what do we really know?)

http://www.adf.org

http://www.druidry.org

http://www.britishdruidorder.co.uk/home.htm

Discussion Questions for Topic Eighteen:

18.1. The author defines three types of Druid in the reading. What are those three types and what distinguishes them from each other?

18.2. What evidence do we have of the ancient Druids?

18.3. What does the author seem to state would be the best kind of evidence for understanding the Ancient Druids?

18.4. What was the focus of "middle Druidry" (the fraternal organizations of the eighteenth and nineteenth century?) What religious groups tend to have that focus today?

18.5. What is the main difference between fraternal Druid organizations of the past and those that exist now but base their organizations on those druids of the past?

18.6. Modern Wicca is sometimes criticized as the fantasy reaction to the horrors of the witch crazes, what could Modern Druidry be seen as a fantasy reaction to?

18.7. Use the recommended reading links to research the alphabet soup of Druid groups mentioned in this chapter. If the author's assertion that Druidry and Wicca are essentially the same with minor cosmetic differences, you should be able to find Wiccan groups with essentially the same statements of belief as those pages.

18.8. Upon what does the author base her claim that Druidry and Wicca are essentially the same thing?

Topic Nineteen: Indigenous American Spirituality

Perhaps more than any other group, New Age writers abuse the heck out of Indigenous American Spirituality. Why do they target indigenous peoples? What should people who are not of those peoples know about this "spirituality?"

Religion, Shamanism, Tribal Faith

Like my research into the Celts, my research into Indigenous North American Religions began as a personal journey. When I was young, I attributed my black hair and olive skin, which genetics, age, anemia and a combination of sun and gray coverage has since rendered auburn and nearly blue-white, respectively, to the bazillionth of Native American I can find in my family tree. Had I known more about the Celts, I would've recognized this phenotype, freckles and all, as classically Southern Celtic, like the surname Morgan. However, I grew up with friends who had names like Ocean and Sky[30], and with people for whom granola and wheat grass were delicious food, not rabbit feed, so it is not surprising that I, raised when and where I was, embraced the sort of quasi-indigenous New Age spirituality one can find everywhere with a happy heart.

I was not a total bunny. I was fortunate enough to have the courage to go to the source for most of my data, gently asking questions of people whose answers I could trust. I thus avoided the majority of the nonsense, but I also came to the realization that my miniscule genetic relationship to the people I met was not enough to shoehorn me into the culture. Not long after that I got involved with my wife, another Celtic American of mixed ethnicity, and the roots we shared became more prominent for us both. Despite that, I have a genuine physical pain at seeing any people abused by New Agers, especially a people I feel any ancestral relationship to, justified or not.

So, even though Native American Religions are not generally considered a part of the broader Pagan community, we have, as a community, misrepresented them enough that clearly some reeducation is in order on our parts. It is with that spirit

---

[30] Both Sky and Ocean where blond haired, blue eyed and pale as paper, but the hippy roots of my community should show here, nonetheless.

that I compose this section. I begin with what I hope is a decent explanation of the use of the terms I will be using herein.

I will avoid the terms shaman and shamanism for describing Native American Religions, in part because, being of an etymological slant, I understand that the term is not accurate, and in part because simple net research will find a number of websites by indigenous peoples in which the terms are described as ugly stereotypes, often established by outside researchers and people with nothing invested in the community they describe. The use of these terms to describe anything beyond ecstatic trance rites and those who participate in them—which certainly does not describe all tribal faiths throughout the world, let alone all those specific to North America—is thankfully becoming less common.

There are those few amongst the peoples I mention who use the term, but I prefer to call people what they'd call themselves if, and only if, in doing so I'm not going about calling a bunch of others something they dislike. This has gotten me in a sticky situation on several occasions, and to that end, I hope that you can forgive me if you feel I'm disrespecting your term of choice.

As for the other terms in this section, I used what I feel was a fairly diplomatic way of choosing my preferred generic term, tribal faith (a term some will recognize from some of my articles on the Celts and Abrahamic religions), as opposed to Native American Religion or Native American Spirituality. I used a search engine to find which definition got me the largest amount of accurate data. Native American Spirituality, as expected, got me the most hits, but by far the vast majority of hits were highly biased writings from outside sources. Native American Religion was a little better, but still full of outside influence. Tribal Faith, on the other hand, returned results of all the similar faiths, both of indigenous peoples of the Americas and elsewhere, and provided me the most links to quality books and websites.

It is simply most accurate, according to this flawed research method, for me to use the term "tribal faith" to indicate the religions, spirituality and beliefs of specific tribes and factions. That I have used the term to describe the faiths of my ancestors and current peoples should be proof enough that my use of the term lacks malice, and I hope the next section will clarify the specifics of the need to differentiate the beliefs at the tribal level. I do not, under any circumstances, consider the word tribe to mean primitive or unrefined, but simply use the term in its core meaning as a social group of affiliated families, clans, dependants and adoptees.

The Myth of the Singular Tribal Religion:

Perhaps the best reason to use the word tribal religion is to distinguish between the reality of the religions and faiths of indigenous peoples and the common myth that there is a grand unified religion, a singular pan-tribal, pan-national religion of "The Native Americans." Many believe this is founded on Rousseau's concept of The Noble Savage, an archetype of "presocial" man that is pretty much complete bunk but still flavors the mood of the day on occasion.

The Myth of the Singular Native American religion states, point blank, that all tribes and nations practice the same exact religion and that the rites are interchangeable and owned by no one. Some versions of it not only teach that all nations are one, but that in the time before the coming of Columbus, all the nations got along and no wars or disputes ever erupted. This is a Disneyesque fantasy as inaccurate as the portrayal of the indigenous peoples as stupid and backwards by the first Europeans in the Americas.

To a degree this myth just comes from careless research. Many books from the eighteenth and nineteenth centuries simply place all indigenous peoples of all continents, under the moniker "primitive" and write of "the primitive psyche" and "the primitive brain" as if indigenous peoples were somehow limited in their ability to think. Others go so far as to speak of a "primitive race" as if indigenous peoples were a different species! Careless researchers, especially in the mid twentieth century, make so much of their rejection of the term primitive that they neglect to change anything else about the old research when they use it and continue the idea that all people who are not their people are the same people.

As if this weren't bad enough, you then get a huge number of people who rush to defend this imagined one nation of primitive people of all cultures who continue the nonsense, but just change the adjectives in use. The "ignorant primitive" becomes the "person of the land who is wise in its ways" and the "primitive psyche" becomes "a mind uninhibited with modern culture." That these are fancy ways of doing the same thing —

dehumanizing a culture of fellow humans and reducing vibrant cultures to an idea of a simplistic childlike ignorance of reality is lost on these people — *they* aren't using the same terms as *those other people* and *they* are speaking of the *good qualities* of the "native person."

The basis for a lot of this, other than the obvious Eurocentricity of its authors, is the same fault we find in the discussions of ancient European cultures, the idea that patterns and similarities bespeak a commonality. Rather than indicating the similarity of peoples and their beliefs, it has to be that these are not patterns or similarities but the same thing. In other words, if two nations share a similar story, it is not the result of transmission or common origin, it is a statement that the two nations are the same nation with "an illusion of difference."

The illusion of difference argument is something people who read historic interpretations of indigenous American cultures come upon again and again. It was the root of the idea of placing rival nations on the same land during the Trail of Tears period, as well as one of the reasons why many nations with peaceful relationships with European settlers were attacked as enemies. It is an inherently racist idea that all people who are not you are the same thing: the other.

The Racism of the Lost Tribes and Atlanteans

As if misrepresenting all the peoples by claiming they are one and the same is not bad enough, another group of people claim that everything, from Cahokia to cliff face pueblos to the pyramids of South America could not have been made by any native cultures because they were "never advanced enough to build such things." These things were made by space aliens, the Lost Tribes of Israel or the Atlanteans. In the eyes of these people, even little green men are more realistic than Indigenous Peoples with technologies and cultures comparable to those in Europe and North Africa.

The term for such a belief is racism: it is the belief that persons of a different skin color are inherently inferior. This may seem a bold statement, but it's actually a simple one. The belief that the people the Europeans found when they got here were too stupid to be the descendants of the people who left behind great monuments — or worse, that the people inhabiting the monuments that were still in use at that point couldn't have

made them is just obnoxious coming from people who forgot
how to make concrete for over a thousand years.

There are four basic theories here at which I take umbrage.
The first two are both based on Abrahamic mythology: the idea
that the Indigenous Americans are the lost Tribes of Israel, Ca-
naanites or other biblical peoples, and the idea that Jesus appeared to them but only the white people know it. In Wicca we
regularly have to make a distinction between objecting to beliefs
and objecting to facts. Since both of these reported facts are embraced by a certain religion (though not exclusive to that religion) I need to reiterate that point: people can object to alleged
facts in your belief system without it meaning they hate your
beliefs or you. It just means you got the history wrong, which,
hey, Wiccans did for over a decade!

To the first, the refutations are numerous. The architecture
dug up by archaeologists bears no similarity to that in the so-
called holy land. The writing systems bear no similarity to Semitic writing systems, and—contrary to the teachings of Joseph
Smith—there is no similarity to Egyptian Hieroglyphs, either,
save the fact that both are pictorial. Genetic findings as well
show the Indigenous American peoples that have survived to
this day just aren't Semitic. To the second, the refutation is solitary but intense: the only people with any "proof" Jesus appeared to the Indigenous Peoples are the Mormons, and this is a
complete shock to those who study the histories of those very
peoples, in which this allegedly weird-looking and magical being just isn't mentioned.

The second collection of tales is equally worthy of skepticism. These are the teachings that all the monuments in the
Western Hemisphere, or at least a good part of them, were
made, not by people who lived in these places, but by space
aliens. To their credit, some of these "researchers" teach that the
inhabitants of these places are space aliens, and others teach that
the space aliens were friends or teachers of the natives, which
explains why space aliens left chisel marks and simple stonema-
sonry tools at these sites.

The last of the things that bug me is teaching that these
buildings and all the good things of the Western Hemisphere
came from the Atlanteans. What immense egos we Eurocentric
types have to paint all good things not of our own creation as

those of aliens, Atlanteans or anybody other than those we have evidence for the existence of. Could it be (gasp!) that people out-side of Europe, the Middle East and North Africa were just as capable of building monuments as people from those areas?

Modern conflicts between modern Pagans and indigenous peoples

In 1993, prompted by a rash of bad neo-native literature and pay as you go instant shamanism courses, especially the works of such notables as Lynn V. Andrews, a group of concerned people created the *Declaration of War Against Exploiters of Lakota Spirituality*, a document that resolved to fight the commercializa-tion and exploitation of tribal rites and religion, by whatever means available. This document was a flare up in a fire long ac-knowledged in the Pagan community — which by that time had already pushed the neo-native movement to the fringe of their community.

This was not, as many subsequent and less virtuous articles by non-indigenous peoples were[31], a condemnation of Wicca, and only the usage of "neo-pagan" in one line could possibly be read in such a way. To do so requires specific blinders but is nonetheless not an uncommon occurrence, primarily by non-indigenous Modern Pagans who decide to take umbrage at it. That line, in the tenth paragraph of the justification for the decla-ration reads:

> WHEREAS individuals and groups involved in "the New Age Movement," in "the men's movement," in "*neo-paganism*" *cults* and in "shamanism" workshops *all* have exploited the spiri-tual traditions of our Lakota people by imitating our ceremonial ways and by mixing such imitation rituals with non-Indian oc-cult practices in an offensive and harmful pseudo-religious hodgepodge;[32] [Emphasis mine.]

It is in the use of the word *all* that most Modern Pagans who identify with the word neo-paganism take offense, reading it as meaning all persons within so-called neo-paganism cults instead

---

[31] The particularly ridiculous "A Wiccan Fatwa" comes to mind immediately, a document apparently aware of neither the nature of Wicca nor the meaning of Fatwa.

[32] *Declaration of War against Exploiters of Lakota Spirituality*, paragraph 10.

of specific members of all of the listed groups. This is the sole mention of any group Wicca is involved with, although some have said a mention of fake "Indian names" applies to Wiccans as well. While I think this is true of some Wiccans, most eke names are in English (as Wicca is a British religion) and in all but the fluffiest of traditions are not taken with the intention of defrauding anyone.

The morass this document denotes was long predicted by the Pagan community. You will note few Modern Pagan groups and associations do not include the words "European" or "Europe" in the description of their bases, and that is simply the result of the tangentially related neo-native movement. Most Modern Pagans are nearly as offended by the neo-native movement as the indigenous peoples it exploits are.

This is not to say that no one in the Modern Pagan Movement participates in exploitive neo-native spirituality, as it is certain some people do. In reality, however, such persons are viewed as exploitive by both the communities they lay claim to. These people are the sand in the gears of intra-community communication.

Such exploitive behavior is not limited to neo-natives, however. More grave, in my opinion, is the disrespect regarding sacred lands exhibited by some Wiccans and Modern Pagans. These range from individual actions by disrespectful individuals to several huge faux-pas by well-known Pagan leaders. Mentioned earlier in this work was a ritual led by Starhawk in 2001, in which she and several others performed a "purification" ritual on a road leading to a G8 summit. This road had been purified earlier by indigenous holy men actually affiliated with the land and her act was viewed, according to a spokesman for one of the groups affiliated with the land as "spiritual and cultural trespass.[33]" The spokesman admitted that some of the protesters had apologized, but in general expressed discontent in the simple fact that people from outside the land would even consider a rite, no matter how small, without asking permission first.

This abuse of the basic concept of guestright is so infuriating to me, and so impossible for me to understand that I cannot dis-

[33] Peter Wesley, in The National Post, http://www.nationalpost.com

cuss the event objectively. Nonetheless, I note with wry amusement that some of the worst critics of those who objected to this alleged purification rite are the very same people who object to the prayer "warriors" who have the laughable goal of praying a Christian prayer in front of every house in the United States. Apparently prayers of other faiths are allowed on people's lands without their permission, according to these folks, as long as those prayers aren't Christian.

Wicca's Responsibility to Indigenous Peoples

One interesting phenomena we feel as Wiccans is a perceived obligation to indigenous peoples. On the one hand, we know for a fact that some of the worst exploitive New Age nonsense comes from within our community—admittedly from the *worst* of those within our community, but from our community nonetheless. On the other hand, since our religion teaches us to become in tune with our lives, gods and immediate environment, those of us who do not live on our own indigenous lands recognize the people indigenous to those lands as having a superior body of experience regarding them.

This body of experience must be listened to, sought out and above all protected. It is for this reason that most Wiccans attempt to have peaceful contacts with our local indigenous peoples. If, to use an extreme and unlikely example, a monster comes out of the dark forest where it has lived for a thousand years, we know that the indigenous peoples will have a heck of a lot more knowledge of it than we do. Frankly, they were here first, and as the original stewards of the land, they will inevitably have more knowledge of it than we do.

There is more than just appreciating the people who know the land better than you to our responsibility to indigenous peoples. We must be vigilant for those who approach us looking for them. This is perhaps best expressed as a general willingness to recognize when and where to turn students and other seekers toward other teachers. In other words, a Wiccan noticing that his/her student is leaning more towards tribal faith must try to hook that student up with reputable teachers of that faith, bearing in mind that that student may even be turned away. We should do this with all students who aren't really seeking Wicca. We should send such students off to study magic, Reconstructionism or whatever they're seeking rather than trying to make Wicca a one-size-fits-all religion. It isn't.

Our responsibility to indigenous peoples, then, is the same responsibility we have to all humans, with the added fact that the knowledge of the land that people indigenous to that land have makes not being a nuisance to such people a good idea. In other words, we must not stand in the way of the preservation of indigenous cultures, we must help when it is warranted, appropriate or requested, and we must avoid those things that harm said cultures.

For the most part, Wiccans find no difficulty in avoiding those things that harm indigenous cultures. It only requires knowledge of the historic problems between the two groups and a commitment to tread lightly when dealing with culturally exclusive rites and concepts. In other words, those who do not act like complete morons do not find themselves a part of the problem.

Recommended Reading for Topic Nineteen:

http://www.kmatthews.org.uk/cult_archaeology/

http://puffin.creighton.edu/lakota/war.html
[*Declaration of War against Exploiters of Lakota Spirituality*]

Discussion Questions for Topic Nineteen:

19.1. What is the technical definition of the term shaman?

19.2. To what culture is the term shaman best applied and why?

19.3. What is the "Myth of the Singular Tribal Religion?"

19.4. What is the difference between noticing patterns of similarity and claiming multiple faiths are one?

19.5. What are some of the monuments historically attributed to things other than the people that make them?

19.6. Do you agree or disagree with the author's contention that claiming aliens and the like built monuments in the Americas is racist? Why or why not?

19.7. What is the reasoning behind the *Declaration of War against Exploiters of Lakota Spirituality*?

19.8. Why do *some* Wiccans read the declaration as condemning them?

19.9. What, if anything, is Wicca's responsibility to indigenous peoples? Is it different from, say our responsibilities to any other culture and religion we may not be and if so, why?

Topic Twenty: Karma

What is Karma? Is it the Law of cause and effect? Two-fold? Three-fold? Ten-Fold? Is Karma the most appropriate term for use in Wicca?

Karmas in Wicca

In Wicca, the term Karma refers several different versions of the idea of cause and effect. For some, this term means that as you do good or bad things in the universe, the material of goodness and badness — the energy, if you will — is weighed, measured and returned to you. It can be thought of rather like a scale, with good things happening to you if you tip the balance towards good, and bad things if you do bad.

It happens in this life. While it may pile up and hit you with a whammy, according to proponents of it, it is fairly instantaneous. It may even be pre-emptive, warning you that if you continue on your path you will come to a bad end. It encourages you to do good rather than evil for the simple reason that if you do bad stuff, bad things will happen to you.

The above is just a share of the Karmas believed within Wicca. The fact that no hard and singular definition of such Karma exists should stand out as a warning sign to you. It seems that in Wicca the word "Karma" applies to just about anything that expresses a relationship between cause and effect. Such fuzzy discussion is always problematic — but it is even more so in the fast-growing world of Wicca. Too often, we think we know what someone else is talking about and we don't.

So what do Wiccans believe about cause and effect? In general, Wiccans believe three main things. First, we do not believe in predestination. In other words, the stars, the moon, your mom, your dad and your genetics do not mandate what you are and what you will become. Some of these things may influence you, but they do not, under any circumstances, *mandate* what you are. From a purely biological standpoint, for example, recombination even means that dominant genes carried by good old mom and dad still might not affect you. Taking the pseudo-sciences into consideration, this means, frankly, that stars and the like don't mean a hill of beans to who you are and what you decide to do.

Secondly, since Wiccans do not believe in predestination, Wiccans believe that the Universe functions with a high degree of randomness. In other words, a significant number of events will happen to you as nothing more or less than the luck of the draw. Thus, cause and effect relationships are affected by randomness, and can seen as affecting the probability of things, not necessarily as *causing* things.

Lastly, since Wiccans believe in randomness and no predestination, it may be surprising to find out that Wiccans generally believe that what they do in the world has an effect. The difference between Wiccan cause and effect and other forms of the concept is that, as described earlier, Wiccans see these cause and effects as changing probabilities, not as having definite singular causes.

It's difficult to understand outside of metaphor, but imagine for a moment that there was a connection between dancing around in your backyard and rainfall occurring. On any given day above freezing in the area I grew up, *excluding* weather conditions, there is a 60% chance of rain, and during certain weather patterns, it rises to as high as 100% and as low as 10%. So imagine, for a moment, that this was a day in which raw probability led to a 75% chance of rain. My imagined rain ritual would add, for example, 20% to that probability, so that instead of a 75% chance of rain, there was a 90% chance of rain.

I could test this, by doing the ritual on days with a 75% chance of rain. If my ritual really added 20% to this chance, observation should show it: in one hundred days, something like 90 should've resulted in rain, with the actual number closer to 90% the larger my sample. This is the main concept of probability alteration, something most practitioners of magic, and some practitioners of Wicca, use often. Personally, I am more pragmatic. If I want rain, a 75% chance is good enough.

This isn't to say that there aren't Wiccans who believe in predestination, that everything they do will result in a specific effect—only that those beliefs don't come from Wicca. Wiccans who are also astrologists, for example, will freely say that people are what their stars make them, and research, anecdote and the like contrary to their views may be attacked or dismissed. Remember: holding all the beliefs of Wicca isn't what makes a Wiccan. *Maybe* it distinguishes a good Wiccan from a bad one, but the lack of a few beliefs, in and of itself, is not a criterion for judging someone as not a Wiccan.

That being said, with a religion so very involved with the blank slate and the idea that everyone who wishes to work can be the best they can be, one must wonder what predestination proponents get from it. With a veritable pantheon of faiths out there, it seems strange to choose one that has historically taught the opposite of what you believe. Such questions, I suppose, are for a better author than I.

Karma in Theosophy

The Theosophical Society was founded in 1875 as a quasi-religious organization which focused on terribly westernized notions of Vedic concepts. It is from Theosophy that Wicca gets the notion that Karma means cause and effect. The word itself means nothing more or less than action, but that's not important to this discussion. Theosophy is one of a number of groups that responded to the evangelical reaction to concepts like evolution by putting evolution into spiritual terms.

The most generic postulation of Theosophy is that man is evolving as a spiritual creature. This evolution is affected both by the Karma of man as a whole and by the Karma of each individual human. In other words, as we move through the universe, our actions cause effects at the personal and species level. That it is impossible in evolution for a singular entity to evolve alone is unimportant. Evolution in Theosophy can very much be thought of as equivalent to the evolution in bad 1950s sci-fi or in Pokémon: the motion of an individual through stages — not, for example, as a change in the allele frequency of a population over time.

While, in a way, the species-evolution half of Theosophy's version of evolution is similar to the idea in Wicca that the Karma of one person can affect another, and is, in fact, similar to concepts of evolution in biology (even if the agent of cause is different), this is inextricably linked with the idea of an individual spiritual evolution. Species-wide spiritual evolution must be guided by masters (called mahatmas), persons who have specially "evolved" in order to point mankind as a whole in the correct direction. It is not the journey of one or two people, but the journey of an entire species guided by one or two people.

HP Blavatsky, one of the prime founders of Theosophy, describes Karma as the "Universal Law of Retribution" and states that it is "the source, origin, and fount of all other laws which exist throughout Nature. Karma is the unerring law which adjusts effect to cause on the physical, mental, and spiritual planes of being. As no cause remains without its due effect from greatest to least — from a cosmic disturbance down to the movement of your hand — and as like produces like, Karma is that unseen and unknown law which adjusts wisely, intelligently, and equitably each effect to its cause, tracing the latter back to its producer. Though itself unknowable, its action is perceivable."[34]

This is the vital difference between Karma in Wicca and Karma in Theosophy. In both, Karma is unaffected by prayers, begging or incantations, but in Wicca, Karma is ignorant. It is merely the reaction of energies to the presence of energy-pull on a rope and the rope pulls back. Theosophy's Karma is intelligent. It guides the world towards a balance of energies. Wicca's Karma couldn't care less whether we are balanced or not — we reap what we sow.

Like Wicca, Theosophical Karma affects us in this world, but unlike Wicca's Karma, it also affects your next life. In other words, a miserable life is a result of past disharmony with the universe. Through no fault of its own, the innocent babe carries the sins of its past life into a new life for atonement. This is antithetical to Wicca, in which all are equal and a bad life is the result of a combination of bad choices and random chance.

On the one hand, the Theosophical idea is easier than the Wiccan one. When bad things happen to us, to know they have happened for a reason, even a bad reason — like being a lousy person in a life you probably don't remember — is more comforting that they just randomly happened. At least they happened for a reason. Thinking, for example, that your country is hated by most people for bad foreign policy is way more comforting than knowing that there are those who hate your country because it is not their country. Even when we meet a racist, whether it's in real life or on television, we want to hear about how he was mistreated by one or two people he is prejudiced against, or that he was indoctrinated by someone else. We cannot deal with those who would hate for completely cosmetic rea-

[34] Key to Theosophy, HP Blavatsky. Online Fragment at
http://www.katinkahesselink.net/other/hpb_key.html.

sons, because such totally random action disturbs us on a deep level. We want to know why bad things happen, and that they happen "just because" is not an answer we accept at a visceral level.

On the other hand, the idea that bad things happen to good people because they were once bad people is simply blaming the victim. If you are hated, it is because you were bad. If you are disabled, it is because you were bad. And if you are poor, it is definitely your fault. While this is no doubt fine in a Christian-flavored, Eurocentric worldview — and is simultaneously related more strongly to traditional Eastern concepts of Karma than Wicca is — it is truly antithetical to Wiccan belief, in which you do the best with the cards you've been dealt, change what cards you can, accept what cards you cannot change, and above all, only place blame where it definitely is. If, for example, you have a genetic condition the problem is your genes, and perhaps in any environmental factors that aggravate it. If you are born poor, as over 90% of the people in the world are, it is not because you were a bad person, but because so many people are poor that you, statistically, are one of them — a problem not with your Karma, but with the world.

Karma in Hinduism and Buddhism

Karma crosscuts the Vedic religions[35], and it is well defined in *The Mahabharata*, the primal epic cycle of the subcontinent. In it, it is defined as the inevitable result of any action taken in one's lifetime. It is paid out in future lifetimes, often multiple lifetimes, as one progresses on the cyclical wheel of existence. It is vital to an understanding of the Vedic religions and their descendants to acknowledge this cyclical wheel. Gods, men and animals — every being, from small to large — moves in a circle. Everything that lives will die, and everything that is dead will be reborn.

The difference between Hindu Karma concepts and Buddhist Karma concepts is nothing more than the differences between the faiths. Both believe that Karma is collected in this life and paid out in the successive ones, even if some of the details vary.

---

[35] I have grossly oversimplified several terms here to make the reader understand the general gist of the concept. I strongly suggest the recommended reading for those who wish to know more.

In traditional Vedic thought, Karma is paid off and dealt with by fulfilling one's dharma, or obligations, traditionally understood within the caste system. To use an easy Western example, if you are born to a family that fishes the North Atlantic for salmon, your obligation is to be the best salmon fisher you have the capacity to be, while being a proper child, then a proper spouse, then a proper parent.

This is quite different from Buddhism, in which the focus is on personal enlightenment and in which one achieves nirvana, which can be thought of as an escape from the reincarnation cycle, by following the eight-fold path. This, history and core differences between the ideas of reality itself are what separates Buddhist thought from Hindu thought, but the real goal here is to see the difference between the shared Karma concepts of these religions and Wicca.

Where these concepts are inextricably linked to the afterlife, those Wiccans that call their belief in cause and return relationships Karma speak of a more instantaneous Karma. When you do bad, you get bad in this life, often immediately. This is problematic to the traditional notions of Karma, in which the whole of your actions are weighed and measured, not any general peaks or troughs in your practice.

On one hand, this is a much more fair Karma, because a few bad days will be well balanced by a lifetime of otherwise good deeds, whereas in Wicca the general belief is that you will be affected by your bad behavior almost immediately. A few bad, selfish days in Wiccan belief and you are smacked down by the universe shortly thereafter. Contrasted with being weighed and measured as a whole, the second seems preferable, but is contrary to the experiences many of us have had at a personal level.

Is a Change in Terminology Warranted?

This leads to the obvious question as to whether a change in terminology is warranted or not. In 333, I mentioned the concept of the historical validity of a word, and certainly the word Karma as defined in *The Mahabharata* has far more historically validity than anything the Theosophists wrote of. The Theosophical view, from which our own Wiccan view grew, has twice the historical validity of that Wiccan definition. From just that point of view, a change in terminology is, indeed, warranted, but the logical question that should pre-date that idea is whether or not Karma is the standard terminology.

In my experience, it is not. While many early authors described the Rule of Three or Law of Return as being "like Karma," an examination of early texts finds very little description of the belief in terms of Karma, and much more of the idea of it being the concept of an equal and opposite reaction. Therefore, we can't truly attempt to phase out the use of the word because it never phased all of the way in.

Nonetheless, some people use the term, and it may be a valid exercise to see if these uses of it gel with the others. Certainly those beliefs called Karma that have nothing to do with afterlives are stretching the term. When a modifier is applied to it — when it is instant Karma, Karma of the present, this-life-Karma or similar terms — that deals with the underlying issues of using the term in that way. However, it also raises the question of why one would use the term Karma at all. We wouldn't call a donut a cupcake because it had powdered sugar on it and that's the usual wardrobe of many donuts, would we?

It does lead back to the previously discussed issue of being as exact as possible when we speak. If an author in the early days of Wicca could say that Wiccans believed that energy worked in ways similar to the idea of Karma — only to find the word Karma applied to these things as if it were actually Karma, not merely "like Karma" — then this speaks volumes about how our community works and how language progresses within it. Perhaps if these earlier writers had stated that it was "like" Karma but "not" Karma, and that it differed from Karma, this would not be a problem... but hindsight is always 20/20.

So while a change in terminology is not necessarily warranted, mostly because the term Karma really isn't being used as a stand alone term in Wicca, but as a secondary term for a tangentially related concept, clarity is something we need. So we find ourselves beating that old clarity horse once more, trying to speak as plainly and as clearly as possible lest we offend or confuse even those people who approach our work in the clearest of spirits and purest of motives.

The Law of Return

This leads us to the concept of what Wiccans really do believe, what it is that we've mislabeled as Karma. This is, of course, The Law of Return. The Law of Return is the baseline belief in retribution or divine justice in Wicca. It is the idea that what one does will inevitably come back in some form or another.

In *Rede of the Wiccae*, The Law of Return is described as the Rule of Three, which has the property three times bad and three times good. This is reflective of an early idea of Modern Wicca — that the energies you put into the world are multiplied by a factor of three when they return to you. In Early Modern Wicca, unlike in the later rewrites of this law, it is a literal multiplication. If energy could be measured, say your circle put a pressure of 11 psi over a 9 foot section of the universe, it would be a direct mathematical equation. Since your nine feet were hit with 11 psi, the universe would hit your 9 feet with 33 psi. It is a mathematical tautology: X-force yields 3X results.

For many Wiccans, this three-fold multiplier just doesn't make sense. It you throw a ball into a wall, the ball doesn't generally bounce off the wall with three times the acceleration it had before hitting. Since our religion follows the hermetic axiom of "as above so below," it is hard for us to accept as definite those things that don't follow the observable nature of the universe around us. We could not really accept that it came back stronger than it left us — but we could accept the fact that it came back.

Calling this the Law of Return is actually an interesting phenomenon because the phrase Law of Return occurred in many works early in Modern Wicca, then virtually disappeared. Later it came back as people began to question the idea of a three-fold multiplier and the use of an Eastern term to describe the phenomena within a definite Western Religion. This tenacity underlies the simple elegance of the term, which offends no one and is uniquely Wiccan. It is a term we needn't redefine or make excuses for, because it is all ours.

The word "Return" can be understood as a short-hand for The Law of Return and a suitable replacement for the short word karma. I have also encountered the words lot, fate, luck, fortune and iteration used in such a manner. I have no way of predicting if one or all of these will be the word used to mean The Law of Return in the future, and expect we'll have to wait and see.

Recommended Reading for Topic Twenty:

http://www.theosophy.org

http://www.katinkahesselink.net/other/index.htm

Any Theosophy Society Texts

The Mahabharata, any translation.

Discussion Questions for Topic Twenty:

20.1. What are the three "types of Karma" found in Wiccan belief?

20.2. What is the relationship between these three Karmas and predestination?

20.3. What is Karma in Theosophy? How does it differ from Wiccan Karma?

20.4. How does Karma in theosophy differ from Karma in Hinduism and Buddhism?

20.5. How does Karma in Hinduism differ from Karma in Buddhism?

20.6. Why doesn't the author think a change in terminology is warranted?

20.7. What is the difference between the Karmas of Eastern Religions and Theosophy and The Law of Return?

Wicca in Practice VI: Approaching a Teacher

Nine Points to Bear in Mind When Approaching a Teacher (J.Tomas)

1. Make sure the teacher is a teacher, and that s/he is currently accepting students.
2. Distinguish yourself from the pack: Explain why you would be a good student.
3. Tell the teacher why you chose him or her: Do enough research to know about the teacher.
4. Be prepared to offer credentials and references, but don't hand the teacher a résumé right off the bat.
5. Respect the teacher's right to determine who s/he can or cannot teach.
6. Remember that the teacher has to invest time and energy in you, and that the onus is upon you to justify that you are worth his/her time and energy.
7. Feel free to be unconventional in your approach, but don't be a jerk.
8. If the teacher has established reasonable policies regarding who s/he will teach, respect them.
9. You are not obligated to being taught by any particular person.

Introduction

Imagine my surprise when I discovered that my usual advice — go and find a teacher — was met with a simple "how?" As stunning as it may be to discover, I had never contemplated for a moment that people might have some difficulty in going about this. When I have needed a teacher, I've gone right in and asked if someone could teach me or not. If rebuffed, I've found someone else, without my self-esteem taking a nose dive or the world coming crashing down around my ears.

Since I am an old-fashioned recluse, fond of mail and email, shy of phones and personal contact, I figured that the way I did it was probably the most obvious of ways. If I could get up the gall to walk up to my teacher of choice, surely anyone could, and they would have about the same results as me, getting taught what I need about 80% of the time, and often, when turned away, finding a better source elsewhere.

Even if I didn't understand the need for a guide to approaching a teacher at first, the more I thought about it, the more I could sort of reverse-engineer the concept, thinking about it not as a student searching for a teacher but as a teacher dealing with students. While I never had a problem finding a teacher, I certainly have turned people away as students, and in talking to other teachers (some of whom were once my students, and some of whom were once my teachers), I noticed there were things that bothered some of us but not others, and things that bothered all of us. From this, I composed a sort of hot-list of techniques that turn off teachers, narrowing it down to six student-from-Hell caricatures.

These caricatures are exaggerated, and don't represent any particular students (even though I give examples of students who have come close). They represent the most extreme forms of the behaviors we see often in Wicca. These caricatures are The Gift, The Waiter, The Lazybones, The Entitled, The Ignorer and The Ex-Student. It my personal hope for everyone that they never encounter these students, but perhaps by reading about them, people can figure out how to avoid them and simultaneously avoid becoming them.

The Gift: "Think of how much better *your* coven will be with *me* in it."

The Gift is perhaps the easiest to understand student caricature. He writes you an email or comes to your classes and, frankly, you're not sure why he's even asking for your skills, or even if he is. In fact, he's too busy telling you he is the gift of the gods to you, personally, for you to figure out *what* he wants.

I met a Gift at a metaphysical bookstore where I was helping a fellow Priestess give a lecture. Mostly I was just watching, handing out paperwork and providing moral support. At the end of the lecture, he blew past the woman I was helping, came right up to me, and offered to join my coven. In the past 10 years, while I've taught teaching circles and worked for The Coven of The Far Flung Net, my offline coven has consisted exclusively of family members and the occasional friend we invite in. He was not asking for an invite, nor was he *asking* if he could join my coven. He *offered* to join my coven, add male energy to my circle, and bring in his extensive experience. He told me, in a two minute speech with barely a pause for breath, that when I let him become my student, he would fix everything that my coven had wrong with it and all-around improve my life.

The problem was, he'd never been to my coven... nor did we feel there was something wrong, nor a lack of male energy. As if that wasn't really bad enough, the lecture had been put on by the priestess of another coven he apparently felt was so substandard that he could blow off its leader, approach the head of another coven, and still get an invitation to join. That's right folks—when I told *The Gods' Gift to MacMorgan Covenstead* that we weren't interested, he walked right up to the person he had already been highly disrespectful to and gave her the same speech, adding that *I* had missed a chance to have a truly powerful member of my coven and now the chance was hers. She passed him up on the offer, too.

The Gift missed a few critical points of approaching a potential teacher or leader. The first was that he misinterpreted the second rule of approaching a teacher—explaining to the teacher why you'd be a good student—as free reign to advertise his *wonderful* abilities and *much-needed* energy. In his entire speech, he did not once explain why he needed a teacher or what he hoped to learn, let alone if he even knew what kind of teacher I was. He was passed up, despite his self-proclaimed abilities just because he was too annoying to even ask for more information. **The Waiter: "But it says if the student is ready the master will appear."**

I've never met anyone similar to this caricature in person, but I have heard horror stories. The Waiter has read, perhaps, The Kybalion and a short book on Wicca, and he's saving up his questions for the master who, Hermes Thrice-Great assures him, will appear the moment he is ready and not a moment sooner. This literalism on his part takes at least one of two distinct forms. In the first, he actively dismisses any attempts at looking for teachers, because he knows one will just appear when he is ready. In the second, he creates an image of what this master will be or what s/he will say and ignores anything that falls outside his idea.

The waiter's main flaw is his literalism and his assumptions, but the truly critical part is the simple fact that if and when his master does appear, ready to teach him, he won't take the important step of simply asking to be taught. He's created this mental expectation that the teacher is out there looking for him… when, in fact, the best teachers are too busy teaching to go looking for students.

The Lazybones: "I was studying under Joe, but it took too much time."

The Lazybones wants to get the benefits of being taught without any of the work. He approaches a teacher with the least expenditure of energy possible, and when and if he is accepted as a student, he promises to do things but never does, whines about being given assignments or chores, and is an all-around pain-in-the-neck.

These people seem to have a sort of disconnect in their logical processes—they have a goal, often a very well-defined, clear goal—but they can't seem to do anything to get to that goal. It is as if they are so focused on their destination they are forgetting to set out for it. What is most maddening about these types is that they often have great potential but just no motivation. They enter the teaching relationship expecting the teacher to provide the bulk of the motivation, as well as the bulk of the work. It is hard enough to teach, even if you love it, without having to also convince your students that learning is worthwhile.

My one Lazybones encounter was as a student, where a fellow student *hated* me for what she saw as cutting her off on the highway of our tradition. We both started around the same time, assigned to work in pairs. She and her partner and I and mine were given regular assignments, and while we did ours, she and her partner would regularly do the least work possible, which resulted in my partner and I getting a bump into the next degree before they were halfway through the first. She hated us for this, and could not open her mouth for weeks without saying something nasty about my work-partner and me. She had the same goals as we did, but no interest in working toward those goals, with the added negative energy of resenting those who made goals she did not.

Eventually, she was coupled with a partner who was very motivated, and to her credit, she soon recognized that her problems in motivation were the source of her issues, rather than everyone else. She figured out that Wicca was a path, not a destination, and turned things around. Lest you fault me for calling the caricature she resembles The Lazybones, that's what she terms it herself.

Perhaps the single lesson from this caricature is that a teacher is expending energy on you and it is simply not fair to expect that, in addition to your teacher's research, help and assistance, your teacher will also do all your work and provide you with the motivation to do it. While a good teacher will motivate you to some degree, as adults, we really are responsible for motivating ourselves.

The Entitled: "You have to teach me, *I* asked you to."

The Entitled is a lot like The Gift, except it is a more insidious personality flaw. It is not merely that their ego is so great that they feel that you will benefit exceedingly from their company, instead it is the belief that you must be their teacher simply because they ask you to be their teacher — often repeatedly.

What The Entitled fails to bear in mind is that the reasons a teacher says no are often varied and regularly not apparent. Until you ask the teacher why, hear what s/he says and understand it, you can never know why s/he rejected you. No teacher is perfect, but most of them do not discriminate against students without a good basis. For example, I regularly turn away students who speak English as a second language poorly and whose primary language is one with which I have no experience. I will generally try to work it out with them, but if I can't understand them, and they can't understand me, it becomes pointless. I will go the extra mile to find a teacher who *has* what that student needs, but if it's not something I can acquire with a reasonable expenditure of extra energy, I will tell the student I just can't do it. In my mind, that entitles *me* to that student's understanding — I have tried and found myself lacking, and where possible found a better person for the job.

Another example from my life was a young woman who was furious I was spending time away from her that she considered *her* allotted time. At the time, my three-year-old son had a stomach flu, and when I told her I just couldn't help her for three days in a row she stormed off and went looking for another teacher. In retrospect, since the stomach bug left me miserable for more than a week later, she deserved what would've happened had she come in and caught the virus herself.

Jayne summed it up best in the last of her nine points: You are not obligated to being taught by any particular person.

Teachers can say no with impunity, and those that do it on unfair bases are the last people you'd want to learn from, anyway.
The Ignorer: "I didn't know that would happen."

I recognize two strains of the ignorer. One is sort of a passive-aggressive Lazybones who forgets assignments. The other, to which this section is dedicated, is the one who approaches teachers while ignoring all sorts of things about the teacher. For example, I used to practice Ceremonial Magic and no longer find it something my life has the time and energy for. I describe myself as a former CM, and tell my students I will help with some core practices, but that I won't teach them CM. Recently, a student of mine decided she wanted to learn more Ceremonial Magic, and the very next time she spoke to me I provided her with a bunch of recommended books and the local phone number of a CM I'd contacted. I'd gotten him to agree to teach her a little, on a trial basis, in exchange for a minor favor.

She, however, would not hear of it, because she felt that she needed to learn from her Priestess. I really had to have a long sit-down with her, explaining that there were energies in the Universe I wished to have nothing to do with, and that I had told her that all along. Eventually, she saw it my way, but she still exhibited signs of The Ignorer.

Most online teachers are familiar with the ignorer. They visit your websites, ignore where you say you don't teach online, or don't teach minors, or don't teach at all… and then email you asking you to do what you have stated you will not. This is contrary to most of the nine points given at the start of this section, but is so shockingly common that it warrants mention.
The Ex-Student: "You're so much better than that *last guy*."

The Ex-Student is a particular peeve of mine. I don't know why I get them so often, or why I encounter the type so often: people who just can't seem to open their mouths without nastiness about their last teacher or their last religion falling out. For my part, I reject such students because I don't want to be the next person they trash to everyone who stands still in front of them, but also possibly because I never really had that feeling of dissatisfaction.

I went to a handful of circles in non-UEW covens when I valued being a part of the wider community over my tradition's limited community, or craved human contact in an area without a UEW coven, often finding them dissatisfying and leaving shortly thereafter. *However,* I never went about trashing them to everyone I spoke to, even if I may have recommended against them to close friends and those who asked. I'm not altogether unsure that these Ex-Student types aren't a personality type, because we see them all the time with other things; they are people who trash former wives and husbands. They are ex-Christians, former smokers and the like.

How to be a good student

We have now gone through a list of what not to do when it comes to being a student. Let's take a few moments to explore the types of things that you will want to do in order to be a good student.

1. *If you don't feel you have found the right teacher, be courteous, but leave and find a teacher who is right for you.*

If for example, you don't believe that Wicca is an ancient religion that has been passed on secretly since before written history began, but your teacher is teaching that very thing, this is probably not the right teacher for you, unless you are simply exploring the nature of a certain coven's or tradition's beliefs. If you're incompatible, be polite, but go and find a teacher you feel you can learn from.

Don't confuse this seeking of compatibility with the refusal to hear anything that does not agree with your worldview. If you disagree with your teacher on the significance of the color purple, this is probably not a reason to find another teacher. On the other hand, if you have fundamental differences you cannot reconcile, you would both be better served by seeking a different arrangement.

2. *If you have assignments or duties, it is polite to either do them on time, or let your teacher/s know that you will be late.*

Be familiar with the guidelines and consequences for lateness within your coven or teaching group. These can vary significantly, from immediate removal to a simple extension of the deadline, granted at your request. If you have duties to fulfill, and others are relying on you to complete them, you must take this into account: while an assignment or essay can be extended, if it was your duty to reserve space at a park for a celebration for your coven, such a thing is not so easily extended, especially if it is now too late to make reservations. Understand the consequences of your actions not only on yourself, but on the people who may be relying on you.

That being said, we all also know that stuff happens, and sometimes you simply cannot turn an assignment in or complete a duty on time for various reasons. If that's the case, please be considerate of your teachers and let them know what's going on. Good teachers are generally very understanding, and will appreciate the heads-up. In the case of a duty, it can be assigned to someone else. IN the case of an assignment, your acknowledgement that you "owe" one frees them from having to write uncomfortable reminders. You may think it's not fun to get them, but I can guarantee you that it's not fun to send them, either.

If for some reason your life becomes so complex that you will be unable to complete your duties or assignments on time in general, having been up front with your teachers will likely predispose them to accept your application later, when you're ready to restart the program. On the other hand, if you simply drop off the face of the earth, they will probably be much less likely to accept another application for the course of study.

3.   *Make sure you understand what is expected of you.*

This seems very obvious, doesn't it? But the fact that is obvious to you and me doesn't mean it's obvious to anyone else. So, this is for all the "anyone-elses" out there.

Knowing what is expected of you and understanding what is expected of you are very different things. Sometimes these can be straightforward, such as being responsible for bringing the cakes and ale to a celebration. Sometimes they're nuanced and subtle, as some reading assignments can be.

Pay attention to incidental instructions, as well. In the example of an essay, if it is not stated explicitly there may still be some clues as to how long an answer should be. In most cases there would probably not be a problem with giving a 487-word answer when the instructions specified 500 words or more. However, an answer of only a few hundred words for a "5000 word essay" or an essay "of substantial length" only proves you didn't read the instructions, or that you disregarded them.

Try to discern if there is a way you can go above and beyond simply completing the assignment correctly. Doing so can lead to new insight on the subject, even if it is one with which you already feel very familiar, and can help you to better understand the expectations of your teacher. This does not, in the example above, necessarily mean always writing a longer essay than is required. It would be better by far to write a more lucid or informed essay than may be expected.

In the example of cakes and ale, perhaps brewing your own ale for a certain celebration, or baking special cakes for the occasion would be appropriate. Think of ways that you can excel.

4.   *Think about the duty or assignment, as well as its implications.*

If you are writing an essay, think about how the lesson applies to your own particular experience. Can you apply the material to your spiritual path? Do you have anything to add from your own experience? Are there parts you would express differently? What do your answers imply about the way you look at the world, and where you might go next in your spiritual life?

If you are fulfilling a duty or performing a ritual, take it seriously. You will not learn as much from something you do by rote as you will from something you do intentionally and thoughtfully. Meditatively and mindfully baking cakes for a celebration is more likely to help you than rushing at the last minute, or baking during the commercials of your favorite TV show.

5.   *Try to anticipate any questions someone may have about what you have done.*

Remember that while you are learning primarily for yourself, you're still trying to demonstrate to your teachers, and often to other students or coven members, that you are learning. If you can anticipate and be prepared for their main questions or reservations, it will make you that much stronger a student.

No one can anticipate everything, however. You shouldn't expect to be able to turn in a paper without eliciting any questions, and you shouldn't expect to perform a ritual or assignment right the very first time. Be willing to accept help and constructive criticism as it is offered. It will show if you've given some thought to these things beforehand, however, and your experience in the course, much richer.

6.   *It sometimes helps to talk about several perspectives on a given subject in addition to your own point of view, because then it can be easier to discuss WHY you have that perspective.*

If there are competing viewpoints on a subject, consider learning about them all, even if you do not agree with them. If you do that, you can take an opposing perspective point by point and explain why you don't agree with it. In the process, you may find your belief is strengthened. You may discover nuances of your own position that you didn't know were there. Or you may discover that the other side of things has many valid points, as well.

7.   *Know where your information comes from.*

Actually, the hardest part of learning isn't remembering the information presented to you. It's determining the validity of the information that is taught. There are no easy answers, here—you simply have to use your judgment.

A good teacher will teach you how to support your assertions: If you state to your coven, for example, that the pentacle is often seen as representing the four elements plus the spirit or soul, you may not need to support your assertion at all. If you make that statement to people who aren't familiar with Wicca, it can be helpful to direct them to a source: an Encyclopedia or a reputable website. If you are discussing the finer points of your religion in excruciating detail, you will be best served to have many sources on hand. A good teacher should be familiar with where his or her information comes from, and should be willing to share it with you.

Some information is based on a tradition's practices. If your coven or tradition casts a circle in a certain, set way, for example, just because there aren't any corroborating sources outside your tradition doesn't mean the information is "bad." However, you should understand, and you should be able to explain to your teacher or anyone else who asks, what is practiced by your coven and if that is different from the way Wiccans or Pagans practice in general. Ideally, you should be able to explain why it is different, as well: what caused your tradition to adopt this method.

If you share something controversial or unusual, remember that your audience may have been exposed to the other side of the controversy, and they want to understand how you've formed your opinions. Part of that will be your description, but a good part can also be looking at the type and quality of your sources.

8. *Don't be afraid to say that you haven't made your mind up on certain issues, yet. You can then discuss the points you're considering and weighing against each other.*

Don't take a position just because you think it's the one you should have, or because you think it's what the teacher is looking for. This is your spiritual journey. If you have questions, ASK. If you're not sure, SAY SO. Sometimes the best discussions come out of poignant questions and serious soul searching. Make sure to examine about your thoughts on the subject, even if they aren't settled, yet. The process may lead you to some insight.

9. *Regard what you have done, whether it is an essay or a duty completed.*

Again, this sounds very obvious, but when you're in a hurry, it's very easy to send something out as soon as you're done writing it, because you just think "Thank the Gods I've finished in time!" It's also easy to believe you've finished with your duties when the largest part of them is over — but the cleanup and administration has just begun. Follow through.

In the case of an essay or written assignment, it's very important to go back and read what you've written because very often, YOU know what you're trying to say, but you don't say it well. In fact, it can be best to write it, let it sit unlooked at for two days, and then reread it to see if it still makes sense, if it's still as profound as you thought it was. It's very hard to edit your own work, and it's especially hard when you've just finished writing it, because your intentions are all very fresh in your mind.

In the case of a reading assignment, it won't hurt to reread it and look for insights you may have missed the first time, or to look at the assignment for logical structure. Does the author make sense? Is he or she consistent? Are his or her sources good? Do you have any questions about the reading that you'd like to ask your teacher?

10. *Double check your work.*

This is your journey as a student. Don't you want it to be the best that it can be? Make sure you double check your work. If you are fulfilling a duty, make sure you've completed it and understand it. Discuss it with your teacher. If no constructive criticism is offered, ask for suggestions.

If you are writing an essay, reread your work not only for clarity but also for simple errors. Always spell check. The spell-checker won't catch everything, but it will catch some of the worst things. So, ALWAYS spell check. When your teacher has read your assignment, ask for suggestions or areas of further exploration if none are immediately offered.

Whatever the case, be willing to accept and address constructive criticism and suggestions as they are offered. If you are unwilling to accept them, if you think you know better than your teacher does—then this is the wrong teacher for you. Or perhaps you are just the wrong student. A good student is willing to learn from those who are willing to teach.

Practice:

For practice, I want you to look over the caricatures and the nine points given and try to write a letter to a prospective teacher. Examine your letter carefully and see if you fall into one of the six caricatures, or come close to it. Once you have it tweaked to your content, imagine you are a teacher receiving it—what does it say that you find objectionable?

For additional practice, I strongly suggest writing in your journal, Mirror Book or Book of Shadows what it is you expect in a teacher or leader. Try to evaluate how many hours a day or week that those expectations will take up and if you could hack that time expense in your life. I found such an exercise, given by my own teacher, to be terribly humbling.

Topic Twenty-One: Afterlives

We return now to actual subject matter of Wicca, the concept of the afterlife, how it is achieved, if at all, and how Wicca deals with the many different contrasting ideas of afterlife.

The Multiplicity of Afterlives

One of the things that makes Wicca different from other religions is a focus away from the afterlife. The idea of what happens after you die, sometimes called The Great Mystery, is something each and every Wiccan is left to assess on his own, with his own experiences and theories. It is not that Wicca states that we cannot know the afterlife, but instead, Wicca teaches that it is not something that can be taught.

This is a pretty drastic change from many of the mainstream religions which tell you that if you do X, you will get Y, with X being some factor of the faith and Y being the promised afterlife. For those deeply steeped in this sort of logic-equation of faith, they are faced with three distinct paths in their Wicca: Change their beliefs regarding how religions and the afterlife are supposed to work, find a branch or tradition of Wicca that promises them an afterlife of the type they believe in or give up on Wicca altogether. I would be lying if I said I didn't consider the first of those three paths the only valid one.

While there are branches, traditions and individual covens of Wicca that will teach about a specific afterlife, most are fuzzy on the idea, either recognizing the afterlife as something to be attained via the completion of a mystery or recognizing it as some sort of great unknown. Some people call faiths with this focus away from death "life-affirming" or "life-centered." While I have some issues with the terms, I recognize what they are trying to say.

Wicca is simply not all that concerned with death. In part, this is because we learn our religion both from elders of the faith and by observing the world around us. We see things die, and things be born, so clearly while death may be the end of us as individuals, it's not the end of the world. The world keeps on going without us, so even if we die, new humans are born and it all works out. Our focus—rather than living life to achieve a good afterlife—is to live life in a way to have a good life. We are concerned with the present and the near future, and with leaving the world a good place for our children and our children's children.

This can be utterly mind-boggling to those with the religious paradigm that focuses on this world as a waiting room for the real thing. The two beliefs are completely incompatible. In one, grace can only be achieved and rewarded in the next life, and the current one is seen as horrible, bitter, harsh, unfair, ungodly, base and cruel. In the other, it is the afterlife, not the current life, which is seen as pretty much unimportant, and the current life is a blank slate that can be written upon as you choose. You can choose a state of grace now or later, and choose to surround yourself with those that do not find this life base and cruel even as you avoid the actions of those who do find it that way.

This is one of the few interpretations of the phrase "Earth-based" that I can agree with. Wicca is focused upon what is happening now, in this place, instead of what is happening in the heavens and in the far future. I find this far more convincing than those whose nebulous definitions of Earth-based make us wonder what planet other religions originated upon. *Wicca is from Earth, Christianity from Venus*, Anyone?

Reincarnation in General

A common belief in Wicca, but still one not held by all Wiccans, is reincarnation. Reincarnation is the belief that the energy of a person — call it the spirit, the soul, whatever — is not destroyed or changed beyond recognition at death. These souls move on to another body and are reincarnated within that new body. In Wicca, reincarnation usually bears more similarity to the process in Theosophy of Transmigration of Souls than to any Eastern Religions.

The idea of reincarnation fitting into Wicca makes perfect sense, and in a way is reflective of the idea that what can be observed in the smallest detail can reflect the larger reality. Imagine, for example, the apple that falls to earth dies, but from which an apple tree sprouts and yields another tree and another apple, and so on, throughout the whole of time. The strict reincarnationist sees that apple as literally the same apple each time it falls, going from life to life, while the more liberal reincarnationist sees a less direct route of passing down taking place.

This is the gist of the divide between reincarnationists. Either, as some have stated, we move literally from one life into the other, with a sort of preserved soul, or our energy is distributed in less direct ways, dispersed into the world at large, or separated into little bits and pieces throughout the universe. As similar as these ideas are, they are crucially different and irreconcilable. If we do not move through the world with a preserved soul — the gist of our personality and experiences moving from one life to the next — the very idea of transmigration becomes impossible. While a fragmented past life memory is possible in the shared-energy paradigm, to have a full memory of a previous life, let alone the concept of karmic debt or moving through a circle of growth, one needs to believe that a bulk of the energy, or at least enough of it to have a cohesive set of goals and experiences, sticks together.

This can cause some pretty harsh dialogs between proponents of the two concepts. In one, the past life has a very strong effect on the present life. Seen at its most extreme, this should result in most of the things that happen to us in this life being a result of the past life, and therefore would eliminate the concept of free-will completely: it happens to us because we set it up that way by our actions in the past. In the other, anything more than a sort of vague regression, fragments of memory that don't make much sense in the grand scheme of things, must be nothing more than one's imagination. In both — though more in the literalist, whole-soul paradigm — the concept that speaking with ghosts, or that souls can remain along after death, or even that ancestors would stick around watching out for their kin is antithetical to their view of the afterlife. If we move on, by definition we can't stay put.

I do not understand how reincarnation and spiritualism can exist in the same paradigm because unless you reduce ghosts to something that could not get closure anyway, you can't say they wander this plane looking for the answers they didn't get in their last life. If they are just echoes or reflections of reality, then the idea that they can be helped across the boundaries into their proper afterlife — the goal of many spiritualist ghost-hunters — becomes impossible. If they are wandering the world trying to find the answers to their last life, surely they'd just reincarnate to do so! For me, at least, the very idea of November's Eve, of the veil between the worlds being thin, cannot exist concurrently with a belief in literal reincarnation. I cannot limit souls to things that can get stuck, nor believe my very active and helpful ancestors have moved on.

This becomes another faith-paradox in Wicca. We use reincarnationist language and spiritualist theology, we talk about the other side and our ancestors, but also of moving on. We have reincarnation, but we also have the Summerland and other paradises. Reincarnation in general often fails us because our experiences point to something bigger. The next two sections deal with two ways Wiccans, who are primarily reincarnationist, deal with those questions.

Non-Linear and Familial Reincarnation and the Ancestral Memory

I have mentioned Non-Linear Reincarnation in all my works because if reincarnation exists, NLR is the only form of it that I feel makes any sense. For those unaccustomed with the concept, the idea is that the soul, or memory, incorporates at any point in time which is useful to that soul, even reincarnating at the same point in time, at different points along the cycle, in different bodies. In this point of view, for example, if being born in 1652 was the only way for you to learn a certain lesson, you might be born in 1652 in more than one body, each time getting a chance to get it right. So, Joe Smith, who is born in 1932 might be reincarnated next in 1652, and next in 1972, and then in 1932 again, but this time as Mary Thomas.

Non-Linear Reincarnation solves several paradoxes. First, it implies that those persons with fantastic visions of the future are actually remembering lives that they had in the past. To use Mary Thomas, above, she might have strong memories of the World Trade Center collapsing, even though in this incarnation, she's born in 1932, and dies in 1978, because last time, she was born in 1972 and died in 2030. She is remembering the future, her visions of her past life in her past in the grand scheme of things, but still in the future in the linear march of time we perceive as a species.

In addition to solving the apparent paradox of those who seem to remember the future, NLR also seems to solve the paradox of those who seem to misremember the past. A person who claims to have a past-life memory of an Avalon, one like that in *The Mists of Avalon,* might not be having a regression that is nothing more than a fantasy-filled trip through imagination, but instead remembering a future world in which someone has created an Avalon.

I am uncomfortable on a deep level with that practice, of saying that memories of the past that bear no similarity to the past are memories of the future, especially when the past is identical to a fantasy novel or two. That being said, I suppose it is more possible than many other things I've found myself believing, and if a person wants to believe that the future looks like a fantasy novel, I suppose it is preferable to those who would insist that, despite mounds of research to the contrary, the ancient world was very much this easy going fantasyland where women ruled with amazing superpowers.

Non-Linear Reincarnation also smashes to bits the concept that population density has any effect on reincarnation. In NLR, since people can incarnate in different bodies in the same time stream, the same number of souls can occupy a large population as a small. Likewise, NLR proponents have a built-in excuse for the people who claim reincarnation must be false because more than one person remembers the same thing—it's all part of the plan.

Related to Non-Linear Reincarnation is familial reincarnation, the belief that members of a family reincarnate within that same family. I mention it as related to Non-Linear Reincarnation because some forms of familial reincarnation not only include it, but make a point of it. A person can be the reincarnation of his grandmother, for example, before his grandmother has passed on. In my experience studying it, it is more common to find what I like to call "small group" incarnation than true NLR in familiar groups. This is the teaching that some small group of ancestors reincarnate within the family constantly, serving as guides of sorts, while the rest of the family are new souls, or souls that are only born once.

Still other proponents of familial reincarnation believe not that the ancestors are reincarnated within the family, but that the knowledge of them is reincarnated, through a sort of ancestral memory. This is not the same as remembering the knowledge of the birth mother, the claim of a completely different set of people, because people who believe in ancestral memory genuinely believe the memories are complete, even if not completely remembered. In other words, even if your grandmother had your mother at 22, the ancestral memory of your grandmother, lurking deep within your brain, would contain all the skills that existed up to her death, regardless of how long after your mother's death that was.

This is why ancestral memory beliefs work more like reincarnation than something transmitted organically. The belief is that as the ancestors die, their memories and beliefs somehow incorporate into the living and stick around, accessible by specific training. This is a branch of the partial reincarnation idea – that the energies are shared and distributed, instead of moving into a whole other body.

The Summerland and Reincarnation

Taken as a whole, The Summerland as interpreted in Wicca is a whole different creature than the PIE concept of the Land of Milk and Honey that existed at the beginning of time (The Golden Age), and which people of exceptional goodness can return to. It is simultaneously a place of rebirth and a place of stagnation in the view of many people, and as most Wiccans conceive of it, quite different than the indigenous European beliefs we sometimes see it survive within.

The Wiccan Summerland is usually conceived as a place of rest between lives, lives that are lessons, stops along that path of transmigration. To stay in The Wiccan Summerland is to avoiding going forth to learn lessons. This is vitally different than the original concept of a special afterlife for heroes and those who died living up to specific virtues, a cultural idea seen in the Abrahamic beliefs as well as most European ones: do good in this life and you will be rewarded in the next.

It is easy to see how this does not always work with Wicca, which tends to believe that what you do in this life is rewarded or punished in this life. It is for this reason that many Wiccans do not believe in hells, yet many believe in heavens nonetheless. From a purely psychological point of view, this is understandable. Most Wiccans are ex-Christians, and it's much easier to give up the bad parts of your religion while keeping the good parts. For ex-Christian Wiccans, the Summerland is often the promise of heaven without the threat of hell.

It's hard for me, for whatever flaw in my psyche, to not roll my eyes at such a concept. In Christianity, there are two basic schools of thought: Universalism, in which no one goes to hell;

and the general belief in both heaven and hell. To buy into the paradise of non-Universalistic Christianity (which is not quite the same as the lack of hell in Universalism), while discounting the existence of its foil seems to me like buffet-table spirituality: "I'll take a little of this, and a little of that, and the context of either be damned."

More palatable to my personal serving plate is the idea of mystery-related afterlives—afterlives which are achieved or revealed through the participation in a mystery rite. These, at least, purport to give you a specific thing in return for a specific action. Rather than *say Jesus' name three times and you'll find happiness*, these afterlife philosophies say that if you do a specific set of things, we'll call them X, Y and Z, you will get a specific afterlife and reward. This is usually a simple bargain: undergo a specific mystery rite, don't kill anyone and don't touch a dead body... or don't eat meat or beans and memorize this speech.

These mystery afterlives relate to reincarnation in a handful of ways. At the most extreme, any belief in them is considered contrary to reincarnation, and any belief in reincarnation is considered contrary to the belief in a mystery afterlife. At the most liberal on one side, reincarnation is the fate of those who fail to do X, Y and Z, and at the most liberal on the other, a mystery assures you a new incarnation. The Summerland (which is not a belief that all Wiccans share) is often up for interpretation between these two camps. For some it is the end result of the cycle of reincarnation. For others it is a place of incarnation. As usual, Wiccans cannot see so subjective a concept as the afterlife in anything but the most general of terms.

UPG and the afterlife

What some may see as a flaw in Wicca, I see as a strength. Wicca does not rely on books or priests to dictate what happens in the afterlife. Instead it relies on UPG—Unverified Personal Gnosis. Wiccans who have had near-death experiences have experienced the same phenomena and imagery as Christians, only with the addition of goddess figures and beautiful gardens. Think what you may about such experiences, that they are a phenomenon of the brain, gasping for air or a genuine visit to the afterlife, but you cannot deny that those who claim such events have strong feelings about them.

In my discussions of UPG I have skirted the issue of communal and borrowed gnosis because I feel that, unlike UPG, these things are absolutely subjective. UPG creates a necessary double standard. You approach what you experience and what revelations you have differently than you approach the experiences and revelations of others. This is an easy and perfectly understandable double standard — a matter of personal history, experience and taste. Choosing what gnosis to believe from others — a vital concept if you intend to take near-death and out-of-body experiences seriously — is completely subjective.

For some, the only external gnosis they find acceptable is that gnosis that falls within their worldview. I agree with this on one condition. If you are accepting and dismissing things on the basis of what matches your personal experience, that sits well with me. If you are dismissing out-of-hand all experiences that don't conform to your worldview, regardless of your experience, I find it difficult to reconcile with an experienced-based faith. How can you expect your own experiences to be seen as valid by others when you reject things for no perceptible reason whatsoever?

As an example, let's look at an imaginary person. We'll call her Stephanie. Stephanie is a former Christian who is now a Wiccan. She is trying to reconcile her former beliefs with her present ones. In an attempt to understand near-death experiences, Stephanie listens to three stories from different people. In the first, a woman she has never met charges her $300 to listen to how she died and found Jesus. In the second, a woman she knows — and who she also knows is concerned about her apparent loss of faith — tells her a similar story about dying and going to see Jesus. In the last, a woman she has never met recounts a similar event when she died — but only at Stephanie's prompting. Stephanie dismisses all three.

The flaw in Stephanie's thinking is that since Jesus appears in all three near death experiences, and she does not believe in Jesus, all three experiences are completely fake and should be dismissed for the same reason. Had she thought about it, she should probably have dismissed the first two, and let the last be. The first two can be easily seen as the result of something other than an actual experience: one a potential lie for the sake of money, the other a potential lie because of misplaced anxiety regarding her faith. It may be that they are true, but they aren't compellingly true. The last woman, however, requires a leap of logic to dismiss automatically.

She has no reason to believe this last person is doing it for any reason other than telling the truth. Agreeing with her doesn't mean she must become a Christian, it merely means that she concedes that this last person believes that what she saw was Jesus. Unless this belief is contrary to Stephanie's experiences, which makes little sense, she should probably accept it. Seeing Jesus proves absolutely nothing. He could be a hallucination, wishful thinking or simply how this particular woman interprets phenomena we'd interpret differently.

Now imagine that Stephanie conceives of the afterlife, for whatever reason, as a great purple room with magenta couches and a deep white plush carpet. She may dismiss the third woman's view of the afterlife because it does not coincide with hers... but imagine she sees a fourth speaker, who tells of the exact thing Stephanie conceives of. Stephanie believes that speaker's revelation because it is communal gnosis—it is more than a single individual's revelation about the afterlife. This goes well with the idea that if a deity really wanted you to believe in something, you would. Stephanie, our good little Wiccan, keeps a journal, just like her annoying priestess tells her to. In her six-teen months as a Wiccan, this journal serves her little, but she does record a powerful dream she has about this afterlife: purple room, magenta couches, bright white rug.

Later, when she hears a near-death experience which is de-scribed exactly the same way, Stephanie writes that down in her journal. She compares the two, and the fact that they are the same tells her more than either the dream or the story could on their own. For whatever reason, Stephanie has been primed by her dream experience to conceive of the afterlife in that way. She may choose to believe this is because the gods wish her to see the afterlife in this way or she may feel that this is a sign to treat this last near death experience with more respect than she normally would.

Since Stephanie shares this afterlife vision with this last speaker, she may chose to believe other things that speaker says. This last thing is known as borrowed gnosis, information, beliefs and revelations given to someone else that you believe for some reason. Borrowed gnosis is the core of the revealed religions. When Moses comes down from the mountain, he carries the word of his god, and gives it to his people. In the Greek Bible, Jesus never writes a gospel. It is all written from the point-of-view of other people. Borrowed gnosis gets less valid the further it gets from the source. By the fifth or sixth retelling, it can be expected that the similarity to the original is depleted. Neil the Wiccan says he sees the image of a goddess on the full moon, and by the time the sixtieth- or seventieth- hand version of the story gets around, it has become "Neil Armstrong is a Wiccan because he met the goddess on the moon."

This is why borrowed gnosis is the most fallible, and becomes less reliable as it goes from the source. Every person must determine whether or not the information s/he is receiving is reliable, exaggerated or just plain wrong. Wicca tends to steer away from borrowed gnosis and teach from the communal stuff while holding the personal stuff as highly relevant to the individual. This three-tiered approach, with the individual on top, many be unique to Wicca in modern times, but was the *modus operendi* of most early religions. Even the huge megafaiths of the Abrahamic pantheon can usually be traced to one person, or a small group of people, claiming to have received special knowledge of which they have no tangible proof.

Recommended Reading for Topic Twenty-One:

http://www.iands.org/ (Near Death Experiences)

http://www.comparativereligion.com/reincarnation.html (Reincarnation)

Discussion Questions for Topic Twenty-One:

21.1. In *Wicca 333*, we briefly discussed the fact that the lack of a definitive stance on the nature of the afterlife in Wicca is one reason why some people do not consider it a "real" religion. How valid is such a statement? Defend your answer.

21.2. What are some of the variations on reincarnation expressed in this topic? How do they differ from Hindu and Buddhist concepts of reincarnation?

21.3. What is the difference between strict and liberal reincarnation, and how do they contrast?

21.4. What are some of the "problems" that Non-Linear Reincarnation solves?

21.5. How is ancestral memory unlike the idea that children inherit memories from their mothers?

21.6. How is ancestral memory a form of reincarnation?

21.7. Why is borrowed gnosis often used in the formation of afterlife concepts?

21.8. How were ideal afterlives usually achieved in ancient cultures?

Topic Twenty-Two: Crystals

Crystals are often associated with Wiccans, and vice versa. Why? What's the big deal, anyway?

Why Crystals came to be a Part of Wicca

Crystals are often associated with Wicca, even though they have no real relationship to the religion. In *All One Wicca*, I even added a small section on crystals and stones because they are common enough in their usage that, in my tradition at least, students wanted to know about them. For me, this lead to an interesting set of questions. Crystals aren't mentioned in Early Modern Wicca, nor in any of the Books of Shadows I studied that were more than twenty years old, yet they are still seen as highly important to many people.

Unfortunately, crystals are often associated with the silliest parts of the New Age movement. We hear "crystals" and we often think of the stereotypical crystal devotee, her ears dragged down by the weight of a pair of crystal spikes, her neck strangely elongated by a veritable albatross of sparkly rocks on silver chains and leather cords, one in each hand, and a dozen more on rings and bracelets. She talks about channeling her energy into the crystals around her. Her amethyst keeps her sober; her garnet keeps her mellow, and her rose quartz fights her depression.

We don't immediately think about all the people who use them in moderation, however, and what these individuals feel crystals do for them... or even how they came to be so common. Crystals weren't commonly used in jewelry until the early 1980s, primarily because the mining techniques to make them widely and cheaply available were not in place. In the 1980s, I had a crystal pendant that ran about thirty bucks, and I can get the same exact thing today for under ten dollars. A nearly identical crystal spear, sold in the early seventies as a geological novelty in a catalog ran over fifty dollars, and all this as the dollar became worth less and less.

The change in price is partially the result of a change in mining techniques, and partially the result of several large finds and mine openings over the past few decades. Quartz crystal, the most common type of "New Age" crystal, is a highly useful industrial material, and many industrial quartz mines carefully extract the purer spires to sell for inflated prices to the jewelry market. Several others offer the amateur the chance to dig through the mine for their own crystals, sometimes for a flat fee. This can be financially beneficial to the talented digger, but is usually more expensive than buying the crystal at a gift shop.

Quartz very rarely appears alone. It is commonly found with gold, copper, iron and other metals as well as with other crystalline materials, including tourmaline and diamond. In the distant past, quartz was often ignored as a pretty but mostly useless by-product of the mining industry. Beautiful quartz loads were often kiln shattered to extract the miniscule amount of gold which they contained. Often this gold impurity in the quartz made beautiful colors that were destroyed by the extraction. The remaining pulverized quartz was a good industrial product, but useless for jewelry and often useless for piezoelectric purposes as well.

We regretted the huge loads of quartz pulverized in the search for gold and other minerals as the use of it in communications expanded. We faced a huge quartz crystal shortage during World War II, and the market is constantly wavering even today, things becoming cheap when a particularly pure load is discovered, and things becoming more expensive as it inevitably peters out. In general, however, it gets cheaper and cheaper as more mines open and the technology gets more efficient.

None of this, however, answers the question of how crystals became a part of Wicca. That is, I'm afraid, a result of what one friend calls the Universal Law of Proximity, or ULP. The ULP works like this: If you sell tomatoes in the vegetable section long enough, the fact that tomatoes are fruits, not vegetables, will be lost to the public. In other words, if you put an unrelated thing near a selection of other things that are related, people will assume that the unrelated thing is related to the others. So, for example, if your shop sells pentacles, athamés, chalices, books on Wicca and crystals, it is only a matter of time before people equate crystals with the trappings of Wicca.

In fact, crystals came to be in the New Age stores, like Wicca, by their usage in a specific community. Crystals go with the psychic movement that Wicca, in part, grew out of. This psychic community, which teaches that the energy of the mind can be stored in crystals (which have a few other uses), suggests carrying them at all times. This leads to the need to sell them… and where better than New Age stores, where the spirit of openness (and sometimes gullibility) allows Wicca to thrive as well?

Man's Love of Architecture

The Wiccan fascination with crystals bespeaks a deeper fascination that transcends religion and crystals—humankind's apparent love of architecture. As humans we cannot help but be fascinated by complex and repeating shapes. Honeycombs, spider webs and the complex patterns of frost on glass figure prominently in our legends and lore, and we obsess upon patterns, real or imagined, wherever they happen.

Crystals feed this love of architecture and basic geometry in two ways. On the most basic of levels, they usually represent sharp geometric figures in nature, the very nature we tend to see as curved and soft. Trees don't form strict forty-five degree angles to each other, blades of grass don't form a thousand perfect triangles, and snow doesn't fall in neat cubes. Nature, as we usually perceive it, is rounded, softened, curved, with few straight lines and few perfect angles. Yet crystals are natural angles and lines—spikes amid gentle mounds, pyramids in a world of vaguely ovoid masses.

This has led them to hold a special place in our literature—masses of naturally occurring geometric crystals are interpreted by their early discoverers as the weapons, dice and bones of the gods, their shapes so incongruous with the world as interpreted by early peoples as to demand metaphysical explanations for their existence. Before we knew a thing about them, crystals were magical, and the moment we learned more they became more so.

The unseen part of crystalline architecture, perhaps understood at an intuitive level even before we grasped atomic theory, is that each crystal consists of atoms arranged in a crystalline lattice. Shatter a crystal of pure quartz with a hammer and you get smaller crystals, shatter those and you get smaller crystals, shatter those… you understand the point. You cannot hit a stick with a hammer and get smaller sticks of the same shape and nature, nor a normal rock, nor most of the things we encounter on a daily basis. However, a pure crystal forms smaller crystals. Even the dust of those crystals, like the shattered one on the cover of this and *Wicca 333*, seen under a microscope, show the edges and forms we associate with crystals. This, too, we see as

the sacred geometry and architecture of the universe —
something simultaneously natural and supernatural.

For some, the only response to such architecture is to see the
core beyond the gods — the divinity above the other divinities —
as the grand architect of the universe. Sacred Calculus, the language of this deity, the fractal, his/her main tool, and things like
crystals the places where the grand design peaks through. We
see this in Freemasonry, one of Wicca's inspirational elders
(something our founders were influenced by, but not something
responsible for Wicca), and we see it in movements within Wicca
to use the paradigms of physics, logic, music and mathematics to
describe the way the world works.

The most common crystals, and the most common theoreti-
cal groups in Wicca, have patterns of fives and sixes, the five
points of the pentacles and the six faces of the gods in later Early
Modern Wicca-the triple goddess and triple god-and the more
you are willing to stretch the limits of imagination, the more of
these patterns you can find. Add in fours, or threes, or both and
every group above one gains some special significance, but in
my opinion, this begins to defeat the purpose. Every number in
existence becomes sacred by virtue of divisibility, which makes
prime numbers sacred by their lack of divisibility, until, at last,
all numbers are sacred — which is, perhaps the real lesson.

Regardless of such interpretations, our structures and our art
reflect our love of architecture. We are fascinated by lines, angles
and arches: The Pyramids, Stonehenge, towers, castles and sky
scrapers. Those things that fascinate us most that we do not
build, from the Grand Canyon to Angel or Niagara Falls. They
still represent the straight lines and simple angles (as well as circles, semi-circles and arches) that we do not normally imagine as
normal or natural. Since we did not build them, and they are not
vaguely rounded, soft and gently sloped as we imagine most of
nature, we imagine they must be supernatural, places where the
grand design of the heavens peaks through.

The Basic Principles of Magic with Crystals

The term "crystallomancy" is used to refer to the use of crystals in scrying or divination, although crystal magic can be used
for purposes other than divination, and often is. The suffix "-
mancy" comes from the Greek root "manteia," meaning "mode

or method of divination." Of similar etymology, "hydromancy" refers to divination using pools of water or ink, and "necromancy" refers to divination by calling on the spirits of the dead.

Generally speaking, crystals most often used for divination are in the shape of a globe or sphere, and can be any of a number of colors, depending upon the preference of the practitioner. Natural stones are quite expensive, so frequently pulverized and reconstituted quartz is used to make an affordable crystal ball. Sometimes leaded glass is used. The crystal ball of the Queen Elizabeth I's court spiritualist John Dee was smoky quartz, so dark it is said to resemble polished coal or obsidian.

Over its long history, crystallomancy has gone in and out of vogue with mainstream society. Although acceptable at the court of Elizabeth I, in the 5th century crystallomancy was thought to be a tool of the devil, while in the 17th century, it is reported that some priests in Germany used crystal balls on their altars, and instructed parishioners as to the correct prayers to repeat while scrying.

Techniques for crystallomancy vary greatly. Some crystallomancers prefer their stone to be completely clear and without inclusions, although others believe that the inclusions found in crystal balls made of natural stones are wherein the magic lies. Some beliefs suggest that only the pure of heart can access true visions in crystals: thus the early use of children as mediums for divination. It was thought that they were "pure;" while the purity of adults could only be achieved through ritual and fasting.

In modern times, crystal gazing maintains much of the mystery of the early techniques, but without the elaborate preparations. Generally speaking, the process of seeking visions within the sphere consists of techniques used to bring oneself into a trance-like state. Some crystallomancy practitioners see images in points of reflected light, while others see images in clouds that seem to fill the orb. Others simply contact an altered state of consciousness within themselves that allows them to access the psychic or magical information. In this way, the elaborate preparations sometimes used are meant to help affect the visionary capacity of the medium. Regardless of the long history crystallomancy has, however, it is important to remember that it is not, as stated before, a component of Wicca's Original Core Theology. It is only Wicca's connection with magic that has brought the two into such close proximity in the reckoning of many people.

But since many Wiccans have crystals lying about, it stands to reason that they are doing something with them, and those who are not practicing crystallomancy are likely using crystals for other than magical purposes.

Whether you believe in magic as psychic phenomena or merely as the storage of energy, crystals have often been discussed as helpful devices to that end. Rather than extemporize on the right and proper usage of them, as so many have, I prefer to discuss the basic principle and source for the claims.

One basic principle to understand is that a common idea is that crystals are containers. Looking at it from a primitive point of view, we can understand the idea. They are difficult to break, roughly geometric, and often have things imbedded within them — things that often vanish if the crystal is broken. This includes both ocular imperfections — rainbows and stars that vanish into nothing if shattered — and bits of other elements, some so small that they cannot be seen with the naked eye yet, magnified in a clear crystal, are visible and brilliant. From a more technical point of view, many crystal lattices have well defined spaces in which things can be suspended, and the idea that energy can travel and be held in such lattices is not only logically sound but experimentally so.

Since the view is that crystals contain things, it's not surprising that we see the idea of crystals as channeling or absorbing energy. As rocks, they don't transmit heat well, so if you grip one in your hand you can feel the heat transferring into the crystal. It is not too difficult to imagine that something that can wick heat away from the body can absorb other forms of energy, but many who believe that crystals absorb energy think of it as a one way thing. I divide people who use crystals in this manner into two groups: the shunters, who channel excess energy into crystals to dissipate it, and the storers, who channel excess energy into the crystals and retrieve it later.

Let me make one thing clear: I have no opinion on what this energy is, if it works, why it works (if it does) and what the right way to use it is. I am being utterly objective here. Based on books, interviews, teachings, experiences and anecdotes I break these people into storers and shunters, and I have no interest in claiming who is right. That being said, these two groups base their practices on two different and conflicting philosophies. For the shunters, just as the crystal sucks heat from a hand, so it can suck energy from a person, then slowly dissipate the energy into the atmosphere. These people use crystals to stabilize their energy highs and burn off excess.

Storers, on the other hand, use the crystals as containers. They believe that their energy may be stored in a crystal and retrieved at a later date. They often believe that different crystals do different things, that some channel anger, and others channel lust, love, pain and pleasure. They use their crystals to fill in highs and lows in their personal energy. Some teach that the crystals have a one to one function: if you put one unit of energy into the crystal, you get one out. Others, perhaps from the experiences of the shunters, teach that you can add and subtract energy, but that crystals leak, and you'll never get out as much as you put in. Both shunters and storers agree that energy can go into crystals, but the idea of how much, how fast, and what happens to it, varies from person to person.

As if that wasn't complicated enough, there are two more types of crystal magic: true crystallomancy, or divination, in which one gazes into a crystal to see some form of truth, and crystal focusing, which is the practice of using a crystal to direct energy in a specific way. These focusers have a different belief than the shunters or storers. They believe that the magic they put into the crystal can be focused or dispersed, depending on how they use it, just as light can be focused through a lens or scattered through a prism. They see crystals not as storing energy at all, but as something with which energy can be manipulated.

Uses for All Those Crystals in Wicca

Even though the use of crystals in Wicca is not something in the Original Core Theology, a lot of Wiccans use them, and because of that, a sort of Crystal Wicca has developed over the years. I personally have many around my house, but that stems more from my son's amateur geology than any spiritual beliefs. Still, I've gained plenty of information regarding their use, and since I was discussing them anyway, I feel it appropriate to discuss this aspect of them as well.

In general, I note three religious uses of crystals inside Wicca. The first of these is their simple use as boundaries, from using them to mark out the circle to the use of ground stones to trace patterns on the floor. In addition to that, crystals are used as symbols of the elements or gods, with specific stones placed at the compass points and on the altar as part of the casting of the circle. Lastly, some people use crystals in a manner similar to prayer beads, even making bracelets or necklaces with stones that represent the elements and the gods.

It is this last use that fascinates me the most. If the circle exists as an enacted meditation, with each part of the circle representing a change in personal consciousness, a string of prayer beads representing the stages of the circle seems one of the simplest truly portable versions of the rite. A friend who practices this has a small bracelet she is rarely without that she finds comforts her at times when casting the circle is not appropriate, like flying on a plane. She uses the feel of the beads, memories of specific meditative sensations and the focus this brings to her mind as a sort of withdrawal from the noisy, stressful secular world.

She begins with a piece of yellow quartz, which she uses as symbolic of air. She clears her mind, then holds the stone and focuses on a brief visualization of air. She runs her hands, in succession, over 13 spacer beads to the next element, and then the other three elements, thinking of how each interacts with air, the east and beginnings. The stones she uses are the yellow quartz, a red tiger's eye, a piece of turquoise and a sphere of greenish-blue lapis. Spaced between the lapis and the yellow quartz is a small string of beads that represent her conception of spirit: a violet amethyst, a hematite star, pieces of amber, jet and a pearl. By the time she has turned the bracelet over five times, she says, with a pause at a different place each turn, she has reached an *inner* circle.

This is a pretty different conception of the idea of the circle than that of Gardner's Witchcraft. Here it is a mental state that settles the mind and allows one to deal with stress or fear, creating the rituals space at the boundaries of the body. Another friend used a similar technique when in a hospital, laying stones on a tray when he was bed ridden, each stone representing an element or aspect of the circle casting, and using visualization when he laid them down. This sort of symbolic symbol casting is a wonderful modern Wiccan addition to our personal religious toolkit, and if crystals and stones help a person to develop a powerful technique, the fact that they were not original to Wicca means nothing.

Some Thoughts for the Collector

Much is written on cleansing crystals and avoiding negative energy in them, and I have no desire to reiterate such writings, both because I find many of them silly and because I genuinely have no desire to make suggestions as to what "proper" crystal usage is. Collecting crystals can be rewarding and fun, whether done for a metaphysical purpose, educational purpose or for no reason at all. There is, however, a downside to crystal collecting, and that's the blood that may end up on your hands if you are not careful.

That sounds scary and a little over dramatic, but the fact remains that while most crystals sold in this country are mined by professionals in safe mines or come from the by-products of regulated industrial mining, a small percentage of crystals come from places where the living conditions, let alone the mining conditions, are appalling. These crystals, sometimes called "blood crystals" can come from countries with oppressive regimes, even modern-day slavery, and very often there is simply no way to know whether your crystals come from these countries or not.

This has led many people, myself included, to primarily purchase stones, crystals and jewelry marked as originating in Europe, The United States and Canada. This can, understandably, limit the variety of crystals that you are using for any given purpose, but it allows you to have some degree of assurance that no one died for your stones. While these blood crystals and gems primarily are the higher end stones, emeralds, diamonds and sapphires, for example, the middle-priced stones often come from the very same places. Diamond mines, for example, nearly always also produce garnets, and often when oppressive regimes have their diamond trade stifled, the garnets and other lesser stones still slip onto the market. Unlike diamonds, which are now becoming well documented as "conflict diamonds" as they come more into the public eye, lesser stones are often ignored when it comes to their sources and who they fund.

This is no little matter. The worst terrorist organizations and the cruelest governments are funded by blood crystals and other conflict stones. As diamonds become more difficult to sell, other stones become the funding source of choice. Already tanzanite, rubies, emeralds and jade have been found being mined in similar manners, and rumors of illicit tourmaline and garnet, two relatively inexpensive stones, have abounded as well.

Pearls and amber too, long viewed as "safer" materials have their associated dangers. In addition to conflict stones, improperly harvested pearls are threatening several aquatic species and run off from amber mining threatens several others. When it comes to pearls, the regulating associations are doing a fair job, and it is my understanding that large quantities of amber found in countries with strong environmental policies have led the worst of the amber mines to be abandoned for lack of profit. This can make every trip into the jewelers or New Age emporium a headache for those of us trying to not fund conflicts or environmental damage.

For me, this leaves me so distraught that I've turned to diggers when I need a stone, and I primarily now work with tourmaline from Maine, which comes in so many colors that it can serve most of my purposes. Other people I know who are concerned with the issue only use gems and stones from their backyard, like the quartz that pops up all over the place in Upstate New York and the turquoise from the Southwest. Some of these people have even established a sort of underground, conflict-free, semi-precious stones trade — trading one type for another.

The only real way to know for sure your stones, crystals and similar things are "blood free" is to harvest them yourself, but since most of us don't have that luxury, we have to rely on jewelers and store owners to tell us where things come from. Many store owners will post this information happily, but many more simply cannot. They buy their stones from wholesalers who buy them from other wholesalers to the point where it is likely that no one knows where they came from.

It isn't a complete loss, however. Many of the more unique pieces and larger stones come with well documented geological notes, so if you're willing to spend a little more money at a time, you can usually get traceable stones. Ethical wholesalers, too, will generally have geological notes since they sell to geologists as well as jewelers. It is, however, yet another thing the ethical

pagan has to think about, and another issue people often don't
know about unless they are informed.

Recommended Reading for Topic Twenty-Two:

http://www.iss.co.za/Pubs/Papers/57/Paper57.html

http://www.jewelrysupplier.com/

http://www.un.org/peace/africa/Diamond.html

Discussion Questions for Topic Twenty-Two:

22.1. How did crystals become a part of Wicca?

22.2. Explain the Universal Law of Proximity. Why is it relevant to this discussion?

22.3. What is meant by "Mankind's love of Architecture?"

22.4. If crystals are natural, why do we see them as supernatural?

22.5. What are some of the rationalizations early man probably made for the existence of crystals?

22.6. Crystals break off in planes… how is this different from most other natural material?

22.7. What is meant by the "intuitively understood" invisible, inner crystalline architecture?

22.8. What are the three magical uses of crystals discussed herein?

22.9. What is the difference between the "shunters" and "storers?" What is similar about them?

22.10. How relevant are the alternative Wiccan uses of crystals to your life?

22.11. Why is collecting crystals "yet another thing" that Pagans trying to live ethically have to worry about?

Topic Twenty-Three: Herbs and Herbalism

How on earth did herbs get into Wicca? Is it another case of the Universal Law of Proximity? What is the Doctrine of Signatures? The doctrine of appropriate treatment? Who was Culpepper? Should I take an herb if I'm sick?

The Wiccan Herbalist

One of the core techniques you find in Wicca is herbalism: the art and science of using herbs to a desired effect. Unlike many other things, the method by which herbalism got into Wicca is well understood. As Wicca was reverse-engineered from existing metaphysical systems and beliefs about the universe that the ancients understood, herbs came along with it. Herbs were studied very early in Early Modern Wicca—understood as a "lost art" that we were rediscovering.

Whether it is a lost art or a continuously practiced one, the understanding of herbs and the practice of using them appropriately is something that has existed in Wicca for more than a half a century. That it probably hinges on the idea of ancient peoples having more of an understanding of herbs than they actually did is unimportant, but we can state with impunity that we know more now than we did then.

Some of our herbal lore handed down from the past, from those ancients who allegedly knew more than history shows they did, is absolutely, 100% wrong. The methods and techniques used to access the powers of herbs were often outright useless, and one of the most common techniques seems so ludicrous by today's standards that it is amazing to realize that it was in use for over three hundred years. Rather than make herbalism obsolete, modern equipment and science makes it fantastically effective, and even possible for those of us who, for whatever reason, cannot grow the plants we need.

Herbalism in the modern age consists of knowing the compounds that exist in a given herb, the effects of those compounds and the appropriate use for those compounds, as well as the best methods for extracting them. We are no longer dependant on guessing and superstition, and with careful work we can even breed for better plants with more of the compounds we need and less of the ones we do not. This change in technique is so striking that some herbalism devotees have books of shadows that look more like organic chemistry notebooks than tomes of metaphysical knowledge and rites.

Still, false herbalism techniques exist, and knowing them, or knowing of them, is often one of the requirements of Wiccan study. For many of these techniques, even their lack of efficacy does not stop the Wiccan from needing to know them. Even those things that do not work at all in medicinal herbalism may be required knowledge for magical uses of an herb, or even for historical knowledge.

The Doctrine of Signatures

The use of active compounds and substitution for similar effects was not always the way herbalism worked. For some reason, many early herbalists followed the outdated concept of The Doctrine of Signatures. This "doctrine," hinted at by Galen and Paracelsus, is best understood, and finally considered as a "full theory," when it appears in the treatise *Signatura Rerum* by Jakob Boehme (1575-1624). Boehme was a master shoemaker and amateur Christian theologist—a sort of part-time monk who believed that he had visions from the Abrahamic god that laid out the grand design of the Universe for him.

One of these grand designs was that the Abrahamic god felt sorry for the plight of man outside of the Garden of Eden so he gave him a roadmap to good health. This roadmap was an indication, upon all plants, of their use in health. In other words, the liver-like liverwort helped the liver, the finger-like hemp helped the fingers, the kidney-shaped kidney bean helped the kidneys, etc. Some of these "signatures" were readily easy to examine, others required careful training and knowledge to spot. The rose, for example, was good for skin by virtue not of its shape, as with other plants, but by the texture of the leaves.

This wishy-washy idea of the sign from god begins to stink worse the longer you examine it. Not only are some of the "signatures" exceedingly silly, some of them are downright contrary. For example, the red berries of the currant mean they are good for the blood, but the red berries of the deadly nightshade are red because they are bad for the blood. Boneset is good for bones because of the shape of its branches that look as if they've been repaired, but no other plant with the same exact shape has the same reputation!

The Doctrine of Signatures is an example of paraherbalism: the pseudoscience in which the use of herbal medicines is founded solely on the basis of nonscientific phenomena. Their colors, shapes, growth patterns and names are used as a basis for their usage, as opposed to trial and error, known phenomena, known compounds and the like. While there are some plants held up as "proof" of the Doctrine of Signatures, these phenomena are few and far between. For every red flower or berry good for the blood there are dozens that are not... and for every spotty or blotchy plant good for a spotty or blotchy disorder, there are hundreds with no effects at all.

So, why does the Doctrine of Signatures stick around? It *is* good for one thing—as a mnemonic. As a mnemonic it can be used to remember the real or fictional uses of any given herb. This means that you use a similarity between the name or image of a plant and its use or type to remember that use or type. So, for example, if you know that rosehips are an excellent source of vitamin C, you may connect the bright orange or red fruit with tomatoes, bell peppers or oranges in your brain. You use the color and shape to *remember* the usage, not to *determine* the usage. One silly mnemonic I use involves the monarda plant, bee balm, which I remember as "My-Yard-A" because I know it is indigenous to where I am from, and won't kill off the native plants.

It is only in this use as a mnemonic that the Doctrine of Signatures has any place in herbalism or Wicca. If you wish to use it as sympathetic magic, in which you do something to the plant symbolically, that's far different from ingesting the plant on the basis of what it looks like. That this understanding is not widespread should shock and amaze you. Never underestimate the public's capacity for silliness, even the public you share a religion with.

Astrology in Herbalism

Another example of paraherbalism is Astrological Herbalism, the association of herbs and maladies with the zodiac and treating patients on the basis of where and when they were born. Astrology is a sticky subject in Wicca. As discussed previously, the Universal Law of Proximity makes astrology and Wicca seem to have much in common, but examined in detail, they are in opposition—one founded in self-responsibility, self-determinism and free will, the other founded upon predestination.

Even though some astrologists will claim they do not believe in predestination, there is no getting around predestination in astrology, whether it is blatant—as in the teaching that people will have specific problems as a result of where and when they were born—or less so, where they teach of "tendencies" towards some characteristics, for example. As if that wasn't bad enough, for every astrologist who swears there is no predestination in astrology, I can usually find one who teaches that there is, so it is not a simple concept to refute. Regardless of its usage in Wicca, there is a strong usage of it in paraherbalism that deserves addressing.

I want to make a distinction here between the use of astrology on herbs in Ceremonial Magic—to decide the appropriate votive offerings and the like for a given ritual—and the usage of astrology on herbs in paraherbalism—to determine the best course of treatment for an herbal regimen. It should be clear by now that I hold no truck with people who base their herbal treatments on anything other than experience and science. I find astrological techniques irresponsible. Every time I use a new herbal treatment, I make detailed notes and I am terribly careful with my quality control. There is no treatment I would use on another that I haven't used on myself *and* of which I have documented the effects. There is not a single herb that I will ingest that I haven't looked up in indices of medicinal and culinary herbs to note any harmful chemicals that naturally occur within them. Ceremonial Magic uses, in which the herb is not ingested, are a completely different issue, and I have no issue with the use of astrology in that manner.

That being said, the astrological herbalism phenomenon bases the cure for an ailment not upon the ailment, but upon a combination of the ailment and the birth chart of the patient. The common claim is that this was the practice of the ancient Egyptians or Mesopotamians, but this is unsubstantiated. In fact, while associating plants with gods and planets is not uncommon, the idea that the medicinal effects of plants are determined by the stars only comes into fashion with Paracelsus, and especially the Puritan Nicholas Culpeper (1616-1654.)

Culpeper was disregarded by the physicians of his own time, but his religious beliefs made him very popular with other Puritans. Thousands of copies of his *The English Physician* (1652) came with the Puritans that settled New England, and it is common belief that this is part of the linkage between Culpeper and the Witches of Murray's Witch-Cult. Since the Puritans were the most hysterical of the Witch hunting sects, it only stands to reason to believe that many of those killed in Puritan witchcrazes were familiar with Culpeper. However, as Culpeper was generally considered godly and a proper Puritan, it is inaccurate to link Culpeper's work with oppression for alleged witchcraft.

That being said, Culpeper, who is the common source for most astrological associations, modern and allegedly ancient, honestly believed, as did Boehm, that his writings were the work of the Abrahamic god. His highly religious work preaches a highly Christian (and fringe Christian at that!) set of beliefs that I find personally disturbing when added to Wicca. Culpeper's sect was hanging and burning its own members for far less than practicing other religions, and personally, I feel that using his material involves energies that I do not wish to have any part of.

The Modern Herbalist

So, ignoring the paraherbalisms, it becomes apparent that modern herbalism requires much more than knowledge of colors or astrological signs. An excellent example of Modern Herbalism techniques in my own life comes from a change I made to a medicinal soup I inherited. This soup, which consisted of a meat stock, barley, carrots, onions, borage and horseradish did wonders for head and chest colds but frankly, no matter how you altered it, it tasted horrible. With a little work on my part, I discovered how the soup worked. The meat and the barley provided iron and a bunch of other nutrients, and barley coats your throat and settles your stomach. Likewise, the carrots and onions were healthy and didn't bother me — the problem was the last two: borage and horseradish.

I tried making the soup without them and it just didn't work, so it became clear that these two ingredients were what herbalists call the "hinge pins" of the recipe. Without the hinge pins, the recipe wouldn't work, no matter how tasty the soup was. I might add that in traditional herbalism the goal is to add herbs to things in order to get them working. The modern concept of taking gelatin capsules of powdered herbs is very alien to the more traditional forms, and anyone who has ever tried to get a colicky child to drink tea can attest to the importance of hiding the herbs in other compounds or coupling them with things like sugar or sparking water.

So my first job as a budding herbalist was to figure out what borage and horseradish did in the soup. I went to the library and read up on both herbs. Borage contained iron, which could be added by using beef instead of chicken in the stock, or by the addition of a small amount of spinach juice to the final soup, as well as vitamins A and C. Since my soup had carrots, borage was probably in the soup for its tannins and malic acid—both of which are good for stuffed noses and goopy throats. However, since I knew sage also contained tannins as well as eucalyptol, an excellent oil for stuffed noses, I replaced the yucky borage with an herb I liked.

This left horseradish, and when I made the soup with sage in place of the borage it worked, but still tasted pretty vile. So, back to the library I went, to see what it was that horseradish was doing in my soup. In fact, I reasoned, horseradish was in a lot of my remedies, which primarily used European plants. Surely there was something there in the whole of the world that worked like horseradish without tasting like horseradish!

So, back to the library I went, to look up what horseradish contained. First, I noticed that horseradish contained thiocyanates, also found in onions; and sinigrin, also found in radishes. So, I increased the number of onions to keep the sulfur compounds about the same, and added garlic, which has similar compounds... as well as several other benefits. Horseradish also has a huge amount of vitamin C and the benefits of all cruciferous vegetables, so I added fresh red bell peppers, vitamin A and C workhorses, and finely chopped fresh greens.

When I made the new soup, I noticed it tasted better and worked but didn't quite do the same thing. It lacked the "sweat" that the horseradish gave it. Still, my family ate it, which was an improvement over the original soup. When the next bout of illness came 'round, I decided I'd take a different tack. Since replacing active ingredients wasn't quite working, I'd turn to replacing effects.

Since I'd been fascinated with herbs since I was small, I looked into what I knew about the effects of horseradish. It is a rubefacient, like mustard, so I knew it made the skin warm to the touch. It also was a diaphoretic, which means it makes you sweat. Since the compounds I wasn't *quite* replicating had these effects I needed something else that would taste good and work as a rubefacient and a diaphoretic. I turned, of course, to the capsaicinoid compounds in our friends the hot peppers and— voila!—not only did I have a soup that worked (in fact, it worked better), I had something that my tex-mex loving family would eat. In fact, they didn't just eat it, they loved it. They liked it so much that several quarts of it are in my freezer at any given time.

Had I followed the tried and true recipe, it would've worked, but since I understood modern herbalism and the best way to substitute, I made something more functional and better tasting. Remedies simply don't work if people don't take them. If you couple that knowledge with a reasonable method of examining the function of herbs, you can find cures or treatments for many of the common ailments.

Modern Herbalism, then, is a combination of research, trial-and-error and examination. It uses the best of science and medicine, personal taste and experience. Above all, it teaches us a critical Wiccan axiom: The proper cure for the proper ailment.

The Right Cure for the Right Sickness

Wicca has taught, from the earliest days, that a strong part of the knowledge of how to treat any ailment is to recognize that each ailment has a proper cure. Magical sickness, for example, must be treated with magical cures, and physical ailments must be treated with physical cures. Therefore, those who train as healers are expected to learn all forms of treatment. They should learn when a psychological or pharmacological treatment is preferable to "energy work."

This is contrary to the teachings of many New Age groups, which will state with a large degree of certainty that energy work can cure everything from AIDS to the common cold, and that if the treatment doesn't work, it is because the patient is blocking or unreceptive. Such nonsense is the opposite of healing, sometimes doing irreversible harm. Wicca teaches a more balanced approach, embracing holisticism.

Holisticism is the idea of treating the entirety of a sickness. When you have a bad cold, you generally have physical symptoms, psychological ones and even spiritual ones. A particularly bad disease, in addition to causing physical symptoms, can make you doubt the very nature of the divine. Those who believe in holistic energy work believe that healing energy, in addition to all the other treatments, heals one part of an illness, not the whole illness.

The idea is to fight on all fronts. A Wiccan in charge of others, whether as a priest or as a parent, must treat the illness or issue at all levels upon which it appears, focusing not on one or two aspects of the illness, but on the whole thing. In addition, this Wiccan has to learn to be a patient — acknowledging when he or she can't treat him/herself and letting others take over when need be.

Holisticism is another one of those terms that is often used badly. Many people associate holistic treatments with New Age or alternative treatments. The idea many have is that a holistic treatment is an alternative to a traditional treatment. However, in the core use of the word, a holistic treatment is using a combination of things to treat the whole person. For example, for my own arthritis, which I've had to work around since my late teens, I use a prescription daily painkiller (which I actually managed without for many years,) an herbal tea painkiller, stretching exercises, visualizations and several lifestyle changes… from how I sleep (often under an electric blanket) to where I live (an area where the seasons change gradually). In addition, I pray about it a lot to try to understand why I have to deal with this illness, which affects every aspect of my life.

When I leave out any of these treatments, I notice my symptoms get more aggravated. The different treatments treat different aspects of the illness — stiffness, pain, factors that can make it worse, things that slow the progress of the disease, even the depression it can cause (and trust me, it can!). This is a holistic treatment, treating the whole illness and the whole person. What I eat, how I play and what I do is established with a holistic treatment in mind. Even how long I may sit at a typewriter or computer, and how long I can write in my journal, is approached with a knowledge that too much can cause me damage.

Lest I seem like a hypochondriac, each of these additional treatments was added at a different time. Some of them, like switching from diet sodas with caffeine to sparkling water, caused me difficulty. Others, like adding stretching to my morning ritual, seemed natural and were quickly adopted. Even simpler, finding what foods were known to help and adding them to my already diverse diet was no sweat, as I and my family will eat almost anything, from tofu to rabbit.

What this required, however, was determining what the problem was, what the cause was (bad genetics, I'm afraid) and what fronts I could attack it upon. Energy, drugs, teas or lifestyle changes alone were simply not enough. The entire problem needed treatment, ranging from the ones detailed herein to ones being researched — I regularly donate to an arthritis research foundation, for example. This is what is meant by the best treatment for the ailment: I try to treat it completely, in a way that functions on multiple levels.

When possible, herbalism can be a strong part of such holistic treatments, not just through the commercialized concept of taking powders and pills, but through the realistic herbalism of adding herbs and compounds to your diet, right into your food and drink. This treatment, however, requires knowing the problems, knowing the right herbs and their methods of action and using them properly, which is not a matter of mythology, astrology or signatures — but of physiology, botany and chemistry.

Magical Herbalism

Herbs are not used in Wicca only medicinally, only in curing the sick and in various recipes, however. Herbs can also be used magically or symbolically, carried in an amulet or burnt in an herbal incense. They can be used to infuse a ritual oil or to decorate an altar. A lilac bush can be grown outside one's home to ward off "evil spirits." A whole nutmeg kept in the house can represent a happy union or marriage.

In other words, herbs can be used in some of the same ways that crystals can: to channel or store energy. Some Wiccans and Pagans, especially those who are pantheists or who lean toward pantheism, see plants and herbs as self-aware beings. They believe that simply because human awareness uses a different mechanism than the awareness of the earth and the stars, it doesn't mean that the human concept of awareness is superior or even preferable.

Sight, for example, is only one, complex way creatures learn to perceive energy traveling in certain wavelengths; but trees and plants reach toward the sun without the use of such instruments. Likewise, touch is only one, complex way mobile creatures learn to navigate their surroundings. Trees and plants are less mobile, but their roots must navigate to water while their stems may twine around supports. Branches may spread to achieve the best angle to receive the sun or to bear fruit. This is still perception; it is just not human perception.

In this magical view, the trees and the earth speak in a language that we can try to understand. To understand this new language, we try to translate it to our own, anthropomorphizing it enough to give it what we regard as magical significance.

To return to the mundane, in some ways—in very many ways, perhaps—this can be seen as very silly. Silly is okay, however. Most of us grew up being very silly. After all, that was the fun of being children. Living as perpetual children might not be so fun; however, managing to hold on to some of that joy would be a lovely change for most of us, especially those trapped in the corporate world surrounded by people whose only interests seem to revolve around watching the latest reality TV and discussing it at length, loudly, across cubicle walls. All day. Did I say loudly?

Perhaps the best use for herbs in these cases would be to fill my ears with leaves or potting soil... but I digress.

This sort of magical herbalism is often based on the doctrine of signatures mentioned above, and on the idea of sympathetic magic. Thus, it must be pointed out again, it is NOT scientifically based or even very logical. In most cases, it's not logical at all, even based on its own, internal logic. It IS, however, based on a long tradition—of illogic, yes, but a long tradition, nonetheless—and to those for whom the long tradition appeals, there is no reason to abandon it so long as you understand that these sympathetic uses are quite different from real, modern medicinal uses of herbs. I would not recommend taking any herbs internally unless they are viewed as safe by modern science, their sympathetic uses, not withstanding. Sympathetic magic is, in my opinion, much better consigned to amulets, sachets and the like unless it's something safe like basil or nasturtium.

Again, though, this goes to the nature of holistic treatments and treating the whole illness. In using magical herbalism for the sick, its sympathetic magic may be used simply because it is the treatment that works best for the patient; it is the treatment that touches that folded wing of childhood joy, encouraging it to stretch forth. This need not be a treatment for the sick, however. Just as in traditional medicine, it can be a wellness treatment. It can also be a part of your communion with your gods or with the divine. It can be a part of a community celebration, as well.

For example, it's traditional to steep strawberries and sweet woodruff in white wine to serve on May 1st. I do it every year. Medicinally, however, the FDA considers sweet woodruff rather toxic, and safe only for use in alcoholic beverages. It contains coumarin, which is lethal in high doses, and was banned as an additive in cigarette tobacco in 1997. In other words, one can certainly wonder if the sweet woodruff is doing anything beneficial other than imparting the pleasant, seasonal taste of new-mown hay to the beverage. The flavor itself is a joy, however, and a once-a-year treat that will certainly do me no harm. I like the qualitative tradition, and whether or not I am deriving a medical, quantifiable benefit from the practice, perhaps the joy it gives me provides a magical one. What is magic, after all?

So long as you know WHAT you're basing your magic on, and WHY—so long as you know the difference between what has the weight of science behind it and what, like poetry or art, merely gives you joy—there is no reason you shouldn't be able to enjoy both. Just don't make the mistake of claiming science where there is only poetry, or only poetry where there is science as well.

Recommended Reading for Topic Twenty-Three:

http://www.escop.com/

http://www.herbs.org/

http://vm.cfsan.fda.gov/~dms/supplmnt.html

http://www.fda.gov/medwatch/

http://www.quackwatch.org/01QuackeryRelatedTopics/paraherbalism.html

Discussion Questions for Topic Twenty-Three:

23.1. What is a paraherbalism? What two paraherbalisms are discussed herein?

23.2. What is the Doctrine of Signatures. Who established it as a full-blown theory?

23.3. The Doctrine of Signatures is often described as a dangerous theory useful only for sympathetic magic. Why?

23.4. Why are Wicca and astrology at odds?

23.5. What is the method by which astrological correspondences are associated with plants?

23.6. One claim often made is that owning Culpeper's works were grounds for accusations of Witchcraft in Early America. Why is this wrong?

23.7. What is a hinge pin? A diaphoretic? A rubefacient?

23.8. Explain the "right cure for the right ailment" concept. How is this at odds with most energy healing treatments?

23.9. What is a holistic treatment?

Topic Twenty-Four: The Tradition Track Wiccan

What is the Tradition Track Wiccan? What's wrong with making your own tradition!? Why should I follow someone else's tradition!? Are there good and bad traditions? How do I find a good one?

What is the Tradition Track Wiccan?

My own teacher had an ability I would love to be able to emulate. She could take a prospective student and within ten minutes be able to tell the future direction of that student. Regardless of what she felt s/he would do in the future, if s/he was honestly seeking knowledge of the gods she would teach him or her, but she was a quick hand with dabblers and flash-in-the-pan types. Her difficult course of study usually drew off the worst of the lot, but every now and then there were a few that got pretty far ahead before they showed their true colors. Every time this happened, she'd kick herself, apologize to the group and move on.

It worked both ways. When I was younger I was a difficult student in which she found potential. In fact, there were no less than two coven meetings in which I was the subject of controversy and her word for my potential kept me involved. Whether she saw something in me, or I was terrified to not live up to her expectations is unimportant, as I have literally done everything she said I would, from bringing UEW to a new generation of young people to being what I hope is a voice for ethical practice.

I never quite developed her skill with the efficacy she had, but there are a few types that I recognize within my own students, ranging from the person involved in Wicca as a form of therapy to the model apprentice — challenging, personal and someone with a lot to teach a teacher. Of these types, the worst, without a doubt — and worse than the attention seeking showman or the egocentric dabbler — is the Tradition Track Wiccan.

The ultimate goal of Tradition Track Wiccans is to start a new tradition of Wicca, whether they find a tradition that is a perfect match or not. In other words, their sole goal in coming to you to teach them is to take what they like or what is easy from your words, ignore the rest, and found a brand new tradition. They are usually pretty easy to find because before they get to a teacher, they have already founded their tradition. Many times when the teacher says that the tradition has a standard way of doing something, they've already decided their way is better, and they don't bother to study what they are taught.

This is not the same as being an atraditional solitary eclectic — taking a little bit of this and a little bit of that from a Wiccan buffet table. Tradition Track Wiccanism is simple misrepresentation: expressing interest in being a part of a community when there isn't, in truth, any interest. Most of the liberal and eclectic traditions have a pretty strong thread of individualism. Doing things in different ways is encouraged, but first you learn the basics and the reasons why they are done in such a way. Deciding, for example, to cast a circle differently than the way your teacher showed you is far different from deciding that the way your teacher is showing you the circle is not worth learning.

The position these folk put their teachers in is precarious. They must decide whether it is worth their time and effort to teach the student anything at all if that student is just going to ignore it. For example, in UEW, you are supposed to know at least the gist of the history in Murray's *Witch-Cult*, even though it is basically ludicrous. A UEW teacher would no doubt have second thoughts about teaching both the real and mythic history of Wicca if they felt their students were going to ignore the real history of Wicca and become another group of pseudo-history spouting loonies. That doubt gets magnified when the teacher keeps in mind that every tradition has a sort of reputation in the Wiccan community and that these newly created loonies could be telling prospective students that UEW was the tradition that taught them these "facts." This would clash with UEW's reputation as a group of people who know their stuff, even if we are known as being assertive about it.

So, Tradition Track Wiccans — whether with the idea that creating their new traditions will make them famous, that it would give them control or simply that their thoughts and feelings are too deep to be understood by the rest of the mere mortals of the world — becomes a dangerous proposition for a teacher. Do you teach your heart out, knowing that parts will be ignored anyway? Do you bother explaining why you teach a ritual or belief a certain way, knowing that they aren't going to pay attention to how you do it? It is a moral dilemma, to say the least.

Recognizing the Need for New Traditions

Recently, I was involved in a discussion with a person with a hard-gard[36] point of view. We were both lamenting the lack of basic knowledge of many new Wiccans when I came to the realization that ten or fifteen years ago many hard-gards were as hard on UEWwies as we were being on these newbies. Somewhere in the past decade or so, the idea of a good Wiccan ceased being a Wiccan who was three degrees of separation from Gardner and became a Wiccan who was close to the Original Core Theology of Wicca… or, at the least, knew where they differed from the OCT and why. This second distinction is innately fair and is so preferable to the earlier one as to be worth mentioning here.

There is a reason why most people are not members of Gardnerian or other Early Modern Wiccan Traditions. A few decades ago, the reason was assumed to be that the student couldn't find a Gardnerian teacher—or worse, that s/he was rejected by one, and was therefore was a lesser student. For this reason, self-taught students and new traditions were often laughed at or considered lesser traditions by the more traditional Wiccans. Many of these self-taught students did have laughable practices, from honoring the Pre-Christian Irish goddess of the Potato to calling their newly founded group the remnant of a tradition passed on from the Neanderthal.

However, there was a second, and in my opinion larger, group of Wiccans who were not members of Gardnerian or similar traditions for serious reasons. This second group—called Reformed Wiccans or even Protestant Wiccans—created new traditions because they understood Early Modern Wicca but had serious issues with it. Traditions were created that focused more on mythology, that mixed Early Modern Wicca with Jungian Archetypes, that were focused on places other than Western Europe and some that just had so many issues with Wiccan history and liturgy that they ceased to be Wiccan altogether.

---

[36] Hard-Gard: Colloquialism for those members of British Traditional Witchcraft Traditions who object to traditions with looser structures or that they view as too removed from the Original Core Theology of Wicca or their Traditional Theology of Wicca

Each of these represents a valid reason for creating a new tradition. Although I was not there at the creation of the group that would become UEW, I do know that the trad I am a part of was founded with the idea that American Wiccans should not be controlled from overseas, should be run in a democratic fashion, should tread carefully with the indigenous spirits around us and should have a strict streak of scholarship and history. These are all really valid gripes with British Traditional Witchcraft, and it was because of these valid complaints that the UEW tradition functions as a spin-off.

These are huge differences in theology—not cosmetic differences like where the circle starts or what extra holidays are thrown into the Wiccan Mix. The problem, however, often lies in that assumption many make: that given a choice, most of those Non-BTWiccans would give up what they were doing and follow a Gardnerian or similar group in a second. In reality, many of these traditions were created to answer legitimate issues with the beliefs or practices of the groups from which they derived. Those of us in or creating such traditions would not give them up for the world itself.

Bad Reasons for Creating New Traditions

That's not to say that all new traditions are created for good reasons. In general, to justify a new tradition, you need to have a legitimate beef with the old one. In the many traditions in which personalization and a wide range of practices are permitted this can be pretty difficult. If the Pink Unicorn tradition uses a pink altar cloth, and you wish to use a green one, and the tradition teaches that the color of the altar cloth isn't important, changing the color of the altar cloth is not making a new tradition. If you don't like the name, and you do everything exactly the same as the Pink Unicorn Trad, but you call it the Blue Bunny Tradition, you're not starting a new tradition; you've just called an old tradition by a new name. Little cosmetic differences like this are not new traditions, and it is disrespectful of the people who created the traditions for you to claim that their work is, indeed, something else altogether—that their creation is your new opus.

Strange as it is to say it, disliking a leader is a poor reason to start a new tradition as well. Many traditions are not the realm of only one person. If you follow the Pink Unicorn Tradition, but the leader of your coven, Buffy, is someone you do not approve of, there is nothing wrong with looking for a different Pink Unicorn Tradition Coven or, if you are well-schooled in the tradition, hiving off your own. If the Tradition is dependent upon liking the leader, or following one teacher, it may not be a tradition worth following to begin with.

There is a single-teacher tradition with which I am familiar in Southern England. In this tradition, the teacher teaches Gardnerian Witchcraft, often word for word, while calling it something else. Her legitimate complaint was that the local Gardnerian group, for whatever reason, refused to teach her. While she knew a lot from books and from her friends in that group, she was not allowed to be a member of the group. So she formed her own. Properly entitled, her group could be called "Free Gardnerian" or "Unaffiliated Gardnerian" or even "Gardnerian-like," but instead she called it by her own name. Having observed her rites at many levels, I must say that I can't tell the difference between her practices and those of Modern Gardnerians, and those Gardnerians I've asked can't tell the differences either.

So, did she have a legitimate reason to create a new tradition? Yes and no. On the one hand, she *is* a practicing Gardnerian, just not a *legitimate* practicing Gardnerian. She believes that the very system that kept her out is fair, just not in *her* case. She follows the same practices with her students. She even refuses to let most noninitiates into her circles. If she had scrapped the system that kept her out because she considered it unjust — and in my opinion, any other Gardnerian group would've been happy to have her—she would have a valid claim to a new tradition: a reformed Gardnerianism. This, she would hopefully have credited to the true founders of her path, and she would understand where she differed from that tradition and why. Instead, like many others, she calls her tradition something else entirely, and believes that this virtually identical tradition is better than that of the coven that wouldn't have her.

I make a pretty stern judgment call on such traditions, but we have to use some legitimate basis for deciding what makes a tradition, what makes a *new* tradition and what makes an *illegitimate practitioner* of a tradition. If the Blue Frog Trad requires members of its highest-ranked clergy to have a college education except in special circumstances… then is a person leaving Blue

Frog Trad to form the Red Newt Trad — practicing the same way except for the college requirement — is this person forming a new tradition? I don't think so. I think s/he's just trying to get into a position s/he hasn't earned. If, however, a person of Blue Frog leaves it for a new system, maybe based on Blue Frog, but with many legitimate differences, I think s/he is creating a new Tradition.

Let's imagine, for a moment, that UEW, the tradition with which I have the most familiarity, is based on Post-Valiente Gardnerian Witchcraft. If it were, the differences between the two would be in the basic coven structure, methods for gaining rank, the history that is taught, the liturgy in use and the ability of individual practitioners to vary practice. These are not little cosmetic differences; they are a *huge* collection of major differences. The differences exist because the founders disagreed with a lot of things, not a few things here and there.

That's the difference between making a new tradition for good reasons and bad. You must know what tradition you are differing from, know why you are differing from it and know in what manners you do so. The differences must make sense, and they must make staying in the tradition you are differing from an impossibly untenable position. That's assuming you are creating the tradition after having investigated and researched other traditions. Those who are so self-involved as to assume that tradition membership, whether as a coven member or as a solitary, would impossibly cramp their style and therefore make up their practices out of thin air while calling it "Wicca" are something else altogether — a thing not worth discussing herein.

Investigating Other Traditions

Not all traditions require a formal membership. Some are created in such a way that membership consists of reading a book and doing what is inside it. These loose, informal traditions are often very odd in that the authors regularly are members of other traditions, or are fast to promote themselves as the students of well-known teachers and members of well-known covens of *other* traditions. That these people aren't practicing the tradition they are writing about should be of some concern to the reader. If it is good enough for you to get it out of a book, the fact that it wasn't good enough for them should be of note. This is not the same as when people leave traditions to found new ones, in which case they shouldn't be mentioning those former teachers as a play for legitimacy unless their tradition is a reaction to flaws in their teacher's tradition.

Nonetheless, a well-read Wiccan will usually have investigated a minimum of three traditions before they settle on one. In general, there is a right and a wrong way to go about this. I always suggest learning some basic, non-traditional material first, then checking out a few websites and books on all the traditions you can find. Make a list of the things that are important to you in a tradition and go shopping.

Investigating other traditions, whether when shopping for one or to better understand your own, should be done with an open mind, but not without a lack of knowledge. Tell the people you are investigating why you are looking, what your goals are and why you have an interest. Ask a lot of questions, and be aware not just of bad answers to your questions, but of refusal to answer questions. Sometimes the refusal to answer a question speaks volumes about a group or a member of that group.

In addition, if you are investigating other traditions as a member of a tradition, try to see what your tradition says, if anything, both about that trad and about other trads as a whole. If your tradition starts getting defensive and telling you not to investigate other trads, you may've found something seriously wrong with your own. Ask why. A good teacher may, indeed, want you to avoid studying another tradition because at that point in your studies you could get confused… but if that's the case, your teacher should be able to tell you when it would be a good time to study that other tradition, and what it is that could confuse you.

Sometimes, a teacher may warn you away from a tradition because it's a scam or a waste of your time. If that's the case, that teacher should be able to explain him/herself and the opinions begin expressed. I've told my students certain groups were a waste of time and money, and why… but that if they had the extra money and time to go for it. And I've been rewarded by students getting back to me with a "boy was that a waste of money and time!" Newer students, interested in the same group, will get forwarded to those burned by it for from-the-mouth reports, but they get the same response: "Do it if you want; no one will hold it against you, but this is what I think…"

Ideally, you should have a firm idea of what separates the tradition that you practice or are interested in from other traditions. This doesn't mean you need to skim the web searching for the new traditions seemingly created every five minutes, but instead you should focus on those with at least a few dozen members, and more than one coven. It's not that size matters, but the fact that larger traditions are generally more stable. Feel free, of course, to investigate as many as your heart desires and as your time permits.

Creating New Traditions

Sometimes it happens that you've investigated every tradition you can get your hands on, and then you give up and start your own. Note the order I've put those in! I do not feel anyone is qualified to start a new tradition unless they have researched several and decided that none are for them. Deciding that you are a control freak and you need to be some sort of big boss is not a suitable reason, if for nothing else than because few tradition founders or heads are big bosses with the kind of power people seem to think they have. Indeed, most have little power beyond what they teach and the hopes that their students treat what they've taught them fairly.

Creating a new tradition should always begin with two questions. First, ask yourself if what you are creating is Wicca. If it is very far from anything else taught as Wicca and is better called something else, you shouldn't call it Wicca. Secondly, ask yourself if it is, indeed, a new tradition of Wicca, and why you are creating it. Every new tradition should be able to say why it was created—maybe not in three or four sentences, but at least in a few paragraphs.

After you've got that established, try to establish what you are basing your tradition upon. Is it a syncretic, or blending, tradition? Sometimes the needs of life require more than one faith, and you may find it better to take two pure paths than one blended one. This sounds unusual to ears steeped in Abrahamic mythos, but in reality, it is not uncommon for polytheists to practice different rites, sometimes to all the gods and other times focused on one or two. It may be your perceived flaws in existing traditions are the lack of ability to practice additional rites or prayers to an additional god. If there is no conflict between that god and Wicca, there is no reason to not follow more than one faith, each flavoring the other.

Even then, establishing a new tradition should be more than just establishing your personal beliefs. Many people who are members of traditions do slightly different versions of rites and rituals. Even amongst families there are sometimes differences between practices "as a family" and the practices "of an individual member." This is because Wicca is not a part-time religion. Very often family and coven members practice apart from their loved ones, not just because schedules sometimes collide, but because it is sometimes just not emotionally supportive or appropriate of them to do so.

In UEW, we have what are called septs, small groups that are quasi-traditions. They are groups in which the core of UEW is practiced, but with the addition of enough things to make the group practicing distinct from UEW. In many traditions, some degree of variation from the core beliefs and practices is allowed without that group being a new tradition. Often, spin-off groups remain affiliated with a tradition even when they differs from it. This allows a high degree of variation from one group to another while still maintaining a sort of unity. Traditions that allow such variations are a good choice for people who want to do things their own way, but also want to be part of a greater community. There is nothing as helpful as a greater community to learn from.

Very often, solitaries feel compelled or even required to create a whole tradition because as solitaries, they feel they don't fit into a group. These solitaries are forgetting that not all traditions require coven membership, and some can be had just by following the directions in a book. This membership in a greater community is often very worthwhile. Then there is always the path of the atraditional practitioner, who does whatever s/he wants without ever passing it on to another person. No one ever suspects that those atraditional solitaries are in it for power or to get their name in a listing of traditions.

So, to sum up, creating a tradition is a great idea if you do not already belong to a tradition that works for you, if you've researched other traditions and they are not for you and if you are creating it to fill a need in your Wiccan practice that can't be filled in any other way. Creating a tradition isn't so great an idea if you have false ideas about what a tradition is, if you're already practicing a tradition that works for you, or if you want to become famous. It also isn't a good idea if you could be better served by practicing more than one non-conflicting religion.

Recommended Reading for Topic Twenty-Four:

http://www.witchvox.com/xtrads.html

Discussion Questions for Topic Twenty-Four:

24.1. What is the "Tradition Track?" What other "Tracks" do you think there are?

24.2. What is the Tradition Track Wiccan's ultimate goal, regardless of how they start?

24.3. What are some of the bad reasons for creating a new tradition? The good?

24.4. What is meant by a "legitimate" practitioner of a Tradition?

24.5. Do solitary practitioners (solitaries) have traditions? Why or Why not?

24.6. Do all members of a tradition do things the same way?

24.7. What is a sept (in the context of this discussion?)

24.8. Why should you investigate other traditions even if you are happy with your own?

24.9. How should your teacher, if any, react to your investigation of other traditions?

24.10. What should every tradition be able to do, within a few paragraphs?

Wicca in Practice VII: Choosing a Tradition

The previous section made this Wicca in practice section practically obligatory, as it more or less assumes you either have a tradition, or know how to shop for one... but, what if you don't?

How Do I Find the Right Tradition?

There are several questions you should ask as you begin to look for a tradition. First, you need to ask yourself if it's the right time for you to join a tradition. Unless the tradition is of a form where practice does not require membership in a group, you need to know whether or not you are ready to participate in a group. For example, legal minors need to get parental permission, and those minors who do not have permission should be prepared to wait until they are legal adults. People with agoraphobia or other problems involving leaving home or meeting others are probably not going to be prepared to meet with a group. Put most simply, you must be emotionally, legally and physically prepared to deal with group dynamics before you even try.

You should also be prepared to study Wicca. Read enough books to know the basics, formulate questions to ask your prospective teachers and tradition-mates and make sure that if you are coming into Wicca from another religion that you've resolved your former issues with that religion. No tradition is well-served by an angry ex-member of another religion or tradition. You aren't ready to become a member of a tradition if your sole focus is how bad your last experience was.

Assuming you have decided to seek out a tradition and that you feel that you are ready to face it fairly—and with the appropriate amounts of skepticism and positive regard—the question becomes finding traditions at all. You cannot, after all, choose from a list of traditions and pick the best one if you only know of one tradition. Seeking people and traditions out can be a huge journey, and too many missteps can make it frustrating.

If possible, make your first stop the Internet. Several websites have lists of traditions, both of actual traditions and of types of traditions. Admittedly, some of these lists are awful and completely useless. Some, however, are very useful, and it shouldn't be that hard to figure out which ones can help you. If they have actual profiles of the traditions—listing the tradition's beliefs and values — that is excellent. However, the best ones will simply link to the homepages of tradition members, or, in some cases, to the tradition's governing body. These primary sources of information are exceptional things upon which to base your decisions.

So, say you've found five or six primary sources that have piqued your interest. Your next step should be determining which of these primary sources represents something that holds your interest. Perhaps the first, and easiest, question you should ask is whether or not these groups are Wiccan. By this, I mean not only those groups that do not say they are Wiccan but also those groups that say they are but bear no similarity to anything regarding Wicca. Use a fair basis for this decision — perhaps distance from the Original Core Theology of Wicca or even differences between groups.

Once you've decided which of the groups to contact first, there are some things you need to watch out for. I was once asked a trick question, in which any answer I gave would make me out to be, at the least, a liar[37]. Frankly, I responded to the question with anger that that person would try to trick me, and I know no teacher who would respond any other way. Since it was an email, I blocked the address at the server, and if that person wishes to reach me, he'll have to do it some other way. The moral of this is that you must ask your questions with honesty, and state your goals when asking them. Carefully evaluate the responses you receive, and don't be afraid to ask for clarification.

What are some Warning Signs of Bad Traditions?

In general, the warning signs of a bad tradition are the same as the warning signs of a bad teacher. The first warning sign is charging for strictly educational purposes. The term "warning sign" is particularly poignant here, because charging for these services isn't an automatic cause for dismissing the tradition, but it is something you should be aware of. Early Modern Wicca had strong admonitions against charging, and most of the older

---

[37] The question involved oath-bound material that the asker knew that I knew, and also knew that answering *him* about would violate the oaths in question. If I'd said I didn't know, I'd be a liar, if I said I did know, I'd be violating my oaths, and if I'd revealed the information to him, I'd also be violating the oaths in question.

groups share this belief. If a group asks for a fee, you have the right and obligation to know why that group does so, and what that fee is for.

One thing to be aware of is groups that scorn other groups that don't charge. Having to justify charging on the basis that other groups are stupid, lesser or Christian-based if they don't charge should bring you to a screeching halt. The last of these is especially troubling and shockingly common. Many Pagans think that by equating other groups with Christians they can get your sympathy on the basis that there is a high statistical probability that any Wiccans they meet are ex-Christians. This sort of statistical averages-playing is very troubling for those of us who never were Christians, but those who were should recognize it as base manipulation.

Imagine: a group so obsessed with the idea that their charging must be correct that they attempt to link those who don't to a religious group many Wiccans had bad experiences with!

Such a group is a fair example both of the manipulative groups to be wary of and the militant ex-Christian groups to be aware of. Often, secure Wiccan traditions won't mention Christianity at all, except perhaps in a comparative way. Those who bring it up for no apparent reason at all, or worse, those who use it as a pejorative, are best ignored altogether. It takes a lot of work to hate a group so much that you use the name of the group as an insult or to cast a shadow over other people's practices!

Ignoring the militant ex-Christian groups, there are other manipulative groups to be wary of. In general, such groups have "infallible" leadership, a rigid conformation to rituals and orthodoxy and a vicious rejection of outside influence. At the worst, these groups are little groupthink tanks, everyone agreeing with everyone else to the detriment of free thought. Even the best such groups stifle creativity and innovation.

In addition to this, you should look into how much influence over your private life these traditions want to have. Run screaming away from groups that want to interfere with where you work, whom you date and what you eat. This sort of extreme manipulation is the opposite of what a religious body should be doing for you. Admittedly, their advice or concern may be warranted, but when heeding that advice is mandatory for continued membership, you're better off without it, anyway.

Once you find the right tradition, and it's a good fit, you'll know. It may take several tries, but eventually you will find a group or book-based tradition that matches your goals, experiences and beliefs. Once you have, an entire new scope of practice will be opened to you, as well as people with whom you share a common voice. These people are incredibly helpful in that their mistakes and triumphs can help flavor your journey and steer you away from similar pitfalls.

Even if you never practice with a group, membership in a tradition helps you express who you are to the community. In a community where the very word Wicca has become nonsensical in many ways, this third level identity can help you sort through the mounds of nonsense. Even if you end up rejecting your tradition for another or starting your own tradition, the part of the journey you've shared with others will be valuable.

Appendix A: Another Self Test.

These questions represent a continuation of the questions in <u>Wicca 333</u>, they are primarily here for your enjoyment, as a result of the people who wrote me to tell me how fun they found the self-test in <u>Wicca 333</u>. The numbers at the end of each question represent the very arbitrary difficulty of the question, with 1 being easy and 8 being hard.

51. What is the astronomical definition of an Equinox? (4)

52. Proponents of Non-Linear Reincarnation think that one of the reasons so many people believe they were famous people is because they were. How do they justify this belief? (6)

53. What does OBOD stand for? (3)

54. A common urban legend in Wicca is that blowing out a candle will somehow insult the flame. While there is evidence in Ceremonial Magic for the belief that blowing will scatter the energy, what is the *common* practice in Ceremonial Magic for extinguishing candles? (6)

55. Who was Dion Fortune? (2)

56. Why is it impossible for Crowley to have written Gardner's Book of Shadows? (2)

57. Do the Lord and Lady comprise their own pantheon? (3)

58. According to *Rede of the Wiccae*, how many types of wood go in a cauldron? (2)

59. True or False: According to Kelley's channeled communications, the Archangels wanted him and John Dee to "wife swap." (3)

60. What is generally considered the major source of the flaws in Murray's *Witch-Cult.* (3)

61. What is meant by eke-names being "the great leveler?" How is this especially poignant in England? (4)

62. What is a white-handled knife called, and also what is its purpose? (3)

63. What is *thelema* Greek for? (6)

64. What's the gist of the sacred whore archetype? Give an example. (5)

65. Why does the Pentacle used in the circle not have an "up"? (4)

66. What is the awen, what does it mean? (5)

67. What direction does the Wiccan circle usual face last?(2)

68. Is Ásatrú a form of Wicca? (1)

69. Who was "put in charge" of writing new Wiccan liturgy that was striped of the Crowleyesque language? (5)

70. The Maiden, Mother and Crone archetype is often replaced by the archetype of the Dutiful Daughter/Virgin, Wife and what? (4)

71. What were Paracelsus' elementals? (5)

72. Name the most well-known figures imprisoned in the Watchtowers, according to Enochian Metaphysics. (8)

73. While we're on the subject, who built those towers, why and when? (7)

74. According to Gardner, who was his primary instructor? (3)

75. Who founded the Alexandrian Tradition? (1)

76. What's a *theological* deconstructionist? (2)

77. Who was the first one to speak of the Necronomicon? (2)

78. Who or What is Albertus Magnus? (And no, he is not Fat Albert!) (3)

79. Define Wiccan "Modernism." (1)

80. In Greek Mythology, who escorts travelers to the underworld? (3)

81. In Abrahamic Mythology, who tells the first lie and what is it? (2)

82. Where was Mesopotamia? (2)

83. What is the difference between invocation and evocation?(2)

84. What's an ovate? (6)

85. I'm naked, it's autumn and I have a golden sickle in my hand. What am I probably getting ready to do? (4)

86. Why are pigs sacred to Persephone? (1, 3 or 8, depending on the answer you give)

87. What do Arjuna, Apollo and Artemis have in common, other than the letter A? (3)

88. One of the single most infuriating things I have ever seen, personally, was a website on a college server with the phrase: "It is called the Villa of the Mysteries because we have no idea what went on there." Other than my strong feelings regarding Pompeii, why does this annoy me so much? (1)

89. What tradition does the author of this book come from? (1)

90. What is a virtue name, and how can virtue names be used in Wicca? (3)

91. What is the difference between operative and ritual witch-craft? (2)

92. Why do I find it so ironic when people reverse-engineer faiths from Jung's archetypes? (4)

93. What are some of the "dodges" people have used to explain that the "Rule of Three" doesn't *really* mean what it says... and where did these dodges come from? (3)

94. Who is generally credited with first claiming Wicca was "The old Celtic Religion." (6)

95. What do an onion, a pretty pig, a huge bull, a red cow and wine have in common? (3)

96. Who added the predictable "Post Modern Wicca" category to the Tomas Timeline? (1)

97. Why do Wicca and Modern Druidry have so much in com-mon? (2)

98. In Indo-European Mythology, who do you trust more to be beside you in battle: A clever man, an archer or a big dumb jock? Why? (4)

99. True or False: Winston Churchill was a Druid. (2)

100. I'm a big ugly guy with a club and a lion skin, and you see me on some amphora buck naked. Who am I? (1)

101. (Bonus question) Who coined the term "Frankenfaith" and where did it first appear?

102. (Bonus question) Who is generally credited with coining the term UPG and what did it stand for *then*?

Appendix B: One-Hundred Elements of the Original Core Theology (OCT) of Wicca

I have been asked what I personally consider the Original Core Theology of Wicca on a fairly regular basis. It is a very difficult question, in part because some of the earliest versions of Wicca are still oathbound and in part because those of us accustomed to studying it are more used to identifying what is not in the OCT than what is. Any good tradition of Wicca teaches the OCT even if to say that they differ from it. In my opinion, the Original Core Theology is *not* Gardnerian Witchcraft, which has continued to evolve. As if that wasn't confusing enough, on a personal level, I recognize three distinct Gardnerian traditions as well as a later "reformed" Gardnerian tradition which springs much more directly from the OCT than many groups, as well as from a handful of other traditions.

I am uncomfortable with the desire many have to trace their tradition to an original proto-coven because I think Gardner genuinely believed he was reconstructing something that previously existed and thus taught (intuitively, not consciously) that other groups were to be expected. Efforts to trace all groups back to his are not an effort to preserve his teachings but to undermine them. If all groups do, indeed, trace back to his, you prove him completely wrong which, while probably true is still mean-spirited. For that reason I prefer to trace traditions by their divergence from an Original Core Theology expressed in the works of Gardner and other authors of Early Modern Wicca. This makes a lot more sense; I have seen many a trad that is less than two generations away from Gardner bear no similarity to the OCT at all whilst some trads with no tie to him at all are closer to the OCT than Gardnerians are today.

In general, I recognize one hundred original core beliefs that make up the OCT. There are others, of course, but one hundred is a decent round number that is small while remaining fairly extensive. I don't agree with many of these elements of the OCT and many of them are factually incorrect. However, these represent an original core, and are presented for the purpose of illumination and contrast.

Beliefs about the name of the craft and its origin:

I.Witchcraft is the religion of the Wica, ancient practitioners of Magic and Science.

II.Witchcraft is the surviving religion of ancient mankind passed on over an extensive period of time in secret.

III.There was a systematic attempt to wipe out Witchcraft by the Christian church characterized by Witch-burnings and the inquisition.

IV.There are 8 Witch high holy days as described in *Witch-Cult in Western Europe.*

V.There is no real evidence of medieval practice of Witchcraft because their tools were common household implements.

VI.Paleolithic art, as well as stone circles and sacred drawings are all evidence of the ancient practice of Witchcraft.

VII.Mythographic trends and patterns are indicators of the ancient Witchcraft religion.

VIII.Witchcraft represents the natural pre-Christian and/or pre-Roman religion of Europe.

IX.This ancient religion was singular, practiced with minor variants but essentially the same religion through the whole of Europe.

X. Midwives, herbalists and other wise people of the past were probably Witches.

Beliefs about Initiations and Secrecy:

XI.The Christian church has persecuted Witches in the past and is likely to continue to do so, therefore precautions must be taken.

XII.Witchcraft must be passed down from teacher to student.

XIII.A person who has been well-screened and researched may be initiated into the religion by enactment of a rite not altogether dissimilar to that believed to be portrayed on the walls of the Villa of the Mysteries.

XIV.This initiation rite must be performed by someone who has been initiated to this rite by another and so-forth, back to the first initiator, who was shown the mysteries by the god and goddess.

XV. An initiate may move within the coven until he achieves the place of the inner court, whereupon he may learn the secret names of the ancient gods.

XVI. Each neophyte and initiate is given a name by which s/he is to be known to the coven. This name may not be spoken outside the coven, and the person's Christian name must not be spoken within the coven so that none may be forced to confess the names of others.

XVII. Each Witch has a secret name known only to that Witch and the god, given by the Priest or Priestess.

XVIII. Outside titles and names are of no importance to the coven, all titles used within are those given to the member by the coven.

XIX. One cannot become a Witch by any means beyond initiation.

XX. If outsiders ask you of your Witchcraft, deny it, saying that discussion of such things frightens you.

Beliefs about Theology:

XXI. The god of the Witches and the god of the Christians are not the same entity.

XXII. The goddess is beneath the god as the High Priestess is beneath the High Priest.

XXIII. The goddess undergoes a journey in which she reaches the underworld, gains information and is reborn.

XXIV. In the underworld, she suffers at the hands of an aspect of the god and gains knowledge.

XXV. We meet upon the full moons as the ancient peoples did.

XXVI. We do not meet because the moon is full but because full moons are ancient times of gathering.

XXVII. The goddess is both mother and wife to the god (later addition, but very early nonetheless.)

XXVIII. The time from May Eve to November Eve is the domain of the goddess, from November Eve to May Eve the domain of the god.

XXIX. The powers of the goddess and the god are drawn into the priest/esse/s during ritual.

XXX. The goddess is both the initiate and the initiator, the maiden and sacred whore, and the priestess/high priestess is a reflection of that.

Beliefs about the Goddess:

XXXI.The goddess was worshipped before the coming of Christianity.

XXXII.The goddess is embodied in the Indo-European maiden and sacred whore goddesses, and certain of the Catholic saints. To a much lesser degree, she is embodied in all goddesses.

XXXIII.The goddess is primarily the sexual initiator and the initiated, the maiden and the sacred whore or mistress of the god. (Images of the goddess as mother and wife come later in Early Modern Wicca.)

XXXIV.The High Priestess is the image of the goddess on Earth and may speak with her voice during ritual.

XXXV.The primary symbols of the goddess are the bowl, chalice and Earth.

XXXVI.The goddess is the wife of the god on May Eve and the mother of the god at the Winter Solstice.

XXXVII.Christianity systematically hid the images of the goddess within the Saints.

XXXVIII.Representations of Women of power, such as the Delphian Oracle, are symbols of the ancient priestesses of the goddess.

XXXIX.The repression of women in the Christian world is an attempt to repress the goddess.

XL.Distrust of women, prevalent in the Christian church, is distrust of the goddess-power within each woman.

Beliefs about the God:

XLI.The god is a representation of the powers of life and death; he dies in the fall and is reborn in midwinter.

XLII.The god is the font from which the goddess gleans Wisdom in her descent into the underworld.

XLIII.The wisdom begins with the removal of the goddess' sole obstacle to the knowledge of the universe, pride, which is removed either symbolically, as in the theft of precious jewels, or in the form of rape/sacred marriage or torture.

XLIV.The god of the Witches and the god of the Christians are opposed to each other, thus Christians see the god of the witches as the adversary—Satan.

XLV. The god is embodied in both the solar entities of indo-European culture and the underworld deities. This paradox is "resolved" by the notion that ancient peoples felt the sun went underground at night, and therefore solar deities are also underworld ones.

XLVI. Deities of all age-types are representative of the growth the god undergoes through the year.

XLVII. Solar festivals are masculine ones.

XLVIII. The priest is the father and leader of a group as surely as the pantheons are generally led by a male entity. (This is part of VII: a recognition of mythographic trends as indicative of the early practices of the "Witch religion.")

XLIX. The god is best exemplified by the dying king cycle, and as such, images of Christ are reflections of that same cycle. While the god of the Christians is not that of the Witches, the similarity is of note.

L. The mythographic trend of the kings who died with the land is representative of the ancient priest-caste of the Witch religion.

Beliefs about Clergy and membership:

LI. Clergy are contrasted with the Christian clergy: Where Christian clergy hold their allegiance to a greater body, Witch priests and priestesses are primarily allegiant to the coven and the coven from which they sprang.

LII. There are levels of membership within the Witch-cult.

LIII. At the lowest levels are the neophytes, who have been screened but are not yet initiates.

LIV. Above that level are the initiates, who have passed the initiation rite.

LV. Above that are those who have passed through one of the mysteries.

LVI. Above that are those who have undergone successive mysteries.

LVII. At the apex of those mysteries are the priest and priestess who give the mysteries.

LVIII. Above them is the High Priestess who may speak with the voice of the goddess.

LIX. Above her is the High Priest (if any) who may speak with the voice of the god.

LX.Above them both is the Witch Queen, she who has trained the leaders of many covens.

Beliefs about names:
    LXI.Men of the Wica are called Wicca
    LXII.Women of the Wica are called Wicce
    LXIII.Both men and women may be called Witches
    LXIV.Neither use the term warlock, which comes from a term meaning "oath-breaker."
    LXV.Rank, family and class in the outside world have no bearing in the circle.
    LXVI.Each person has a secret name given to him by the gods/High Priestess.
    LXVII.That secret name should not be spoken outside the coven.
    LXVIII.That secret name is inscribed within the coven's unique book of shadows.
    LXIX.That name has a corresponding sigil which is used in its stead when possible.
    LXX.The true name of a person or a god has power.

Beliefs about Magic:
    LXXI.Magic is the genuine manipulation of energies to a desired effect.
    LXXII.It is an utterly real phenomena.
    LXXIII.Magic is the misunderstood science by which ancient Witches did things we cannot explain, such as cure diseases or build great monuments.
    LXXIV.Science is studying the relevance of magic even as we speak.
    LXXV.Magic may be contained within the circle.
    LXXVI.The circle can be used to build the magic, focus it to a particular point and release it.
    LXXVII.This focused point within the circle takes the form of a cone.
    LXXVIII.Magic may be hampered by the presence of certain materials within the circle.
    LXXIX.All persons possess magical energy fields.
    LXXX.The strength of the ancient beliefs were manifest in their ability to use magic at the highest levels.

Beliefs about Death:

LXXXI.Life is a cycle: we are born, grow, die and are reborn.

LXXXII.This rebirth, while similar in a way to reincarnation, reflects the growth into a higher state of knowledge.

LXXXIII.This is reflected in the initiation rite, where one must be reborn to come into the knowledge of the Wica.

LXXXIV.Death is merely a change in state from one form of energy to another.

LXXXV.We transmigrate from soul to soul in a journey toward total knowledge.

LXXXVI.There are those amongst us whose have traveled much further on the path toward total knowledge and have come here to help us.

LXXXVII.Some of the dead stick around to watch over loved ones, and may be contacted.

LXXXVIII.Some of the dead get stuck between worlds and may be understood as ghosts or negative energy.

LXXXIX.On November Eve, the veil between the worlds is at its most thin.

XC.On November Eve, the dead walk among the living.

Beliefs about Christianity and specific Christian figures:

XCI.The Christian church is afraid of the religion of the Wica and actively hunts it out.

XCII.The reason for the similarities between Witchcraft and the religion of Christianity is that Christianity borrowed from Witchcraft.

XCIII.Jesus may've been a Witch — he had a coven of 12 and knowledge of ancient rituals.

XCIV.The confessions of victims of the Burning Times are similar because they all practiced the religion of the Wica — not because they were asked leading questions!

XCV.Joan of Arc was probably a Witch — thus the term Maid of Orleans.

XCVI.The Christian Church regularly enlists Witches within convent walls to mysterious ends.

XCVII.The Christian Church regularly had the wool pulled over its eyes by smart witches, so you can see pagan figures on many churches.

XCVIII.Mary Magdalene was probably a Witch—thus her skill with and access to herbs and oils.

XCIX.The Christian Devil has horns because the Horned God does.

C.Few real Witches lived long enough behind bars to be tortured—they had access to drugs and poisons.

Appendix C: Ten Common Logical Fallacies

I am often put in the strange position of helping people think things through—not just my own family's decisions, either, but those of friends,and neighbors, who seem to think that I have some higher grasp of the Universe than they. What they are perceiving, rather than a higher knowledge or great wisdom, is my own study of logical fallacies. When I was an atheist, these were incredibly important to my day-to-day experiences. Logic and rationality were my gods—which is really, in my opinion, the only kind of atheist worth being.

Logical fallacies won't make you smart, but being aware of their presence in your life can make you a bit wiser to the ways of the universe. For the most part, they depend on conclusions that don't make much sense. In logic, we might say that a logical fallacy is an if-then statement where the "then" is false, regardless of the "if"... or, symbolically, $p{\to}q$, where q is false regardless of the p... but the relationship is still insisted upon.

This sounds more complicated than it is, so I will try to illustrate many of the fallacies I am discussing here as the result of simple $p{\to}q$ statements, or if-thens. For those unfamiliar with this notation, it is one in which the expressed relationship is that q follows as a result of p. For example, if I am drinking, water but I'm still thirsty, and nothing is wrong with me or the water, I'm still thirsty because I have not had enough to drink. So, p is "I am still thirsty" and q is "I have not had enough to drink," or "If I am still thirsty, then I have not had enough to drink."

There are many more than ten logical fallacies in existence. In fact, one of the ten I am presenting isn't really a logical fallacy at all, but an error in construction—one of those things that people who study logic quibble over the logistics of. I have little invested in teaching anyone logic, but the brief exercise at the end of this appendix should explain why I think these ten fallacies are something you should really know.

1. Non Sequitur: Since I am using the $p{\to}q$ format, the simplest logical fallacy is the non sequitur, literally things that "don't follow." These are $p{\to}q$ statements where p and q have no apparent relationship. Using the above, that p = "I am still thirsty," a non sequitur might be that q= "I am wearing a red shirt" or "I am Wiccan." Neither of these phrases alone follow the first one in a way that makes sense. It may well be that I have not had enough to drink because I am wearing a red shirt and locked in a room where people with red shirts aren't allowed to drink, but that would not be p→q, but p as a result of q and a lot more. The non sequitur reads "If I am still thirsty, then I am wearing a red shirt," which is probably nonsensical, and in situations where it is not, requires more info to be considered true.

2. Not enough information: Some people object to this being labeled a logical fallacy, because in reality, it's an error in the construction of an argument. Above, "If I am still thirsty, then I am wearing a red shirt" is probably a non sequitur, but it could be not enough information. Imagine this situation: During a long tag-team footrace, everyone is given two shirts to wear over their normal clothes — a yellow one that says you need to be replaced by your teammate in the next lap, and a red one that says you need to have water brought out to you. In this situation, *If I am still thirsty, then I am wearing a red shirt* may well be true, and it is probably true in reverse, but without the additional information, the statement makes no sense. We see this a lot on message boards and in chat rooms where the lack of additional information in a text format (without tone, feeling or mood) leads to false conclusions about what is said. The not-enough-information error comes in two basic types: the assumption of error because of lack of data, and the assumption of error because of the addition of other unrelated or false data. If I could change one thing in the universe, this second category would be it!

3. Error of Conclusion: More than a fallacy, error of conclusion is a special type of non sequitur where there is a relationship between p and q, but the relationship is not causal, in other words, it is the statement that if p then q, even though it may well be that p→r and r→q or an even more complicated concept. One of my favorite examples uses the fact that most well-off persons in the United States send their children to college, and the related fact that most of the indoor swimming pools that are privately-owned are owned by the most well to do people of all. The conclusion? Well, if you own an indoor pool, then your children will go to college. This fallacy is also called mistaking correlation with causation and is often used in news stories to make people feel strongly toward a particular thing. For example, people who eat a large variety of green leafy vegetables tend to have more money and higher levels of education, and the wonders of eating a large variety of green leafy vegetables is often portrayed way beyond its usefulness. In fact, being poor and poorly educated, will probably affect your health about the same whether you eat four types of green leafy vegetables or thirty.

4. Relativism: This is a huge one for any group that relies on UPG, because relativism is the "but not for me" fallacy. Where it differs from UPG is when it is used to discuss facts, not opinions or beliefs. This can be understood as if p then q, but only for a specific person or group. For example, if Joe had an encounter with Zeus, and Zeus said he'd given up on lightning and now was a god of hail, that would be UPG, and he'd be fine with it. If, however, he then tried to parlay this UPG into an argument against facts, then Joe would be engaging in a fallacy. For example, Joe is not making an error in logic if he says that Zeus is a god of lightning but not for him, or that Zeus was a god of lightning to the ancient Greeks but not to him… but he is if he states that, to him, Zeus was not a god of lightning to the ancient Greeks. This can be a difficult thing to understand, but it comes down to whether or not the thing being discussed is a relative quantity. In an objective situation — for example that any number multiplied by one is equal to itself — relativism is always wrong. If your belief is that 1x3=4, it doesn't mean that 1x3=4 is true for you, but not for everyone else — it means that your belief is contrary to the facts.

5. The Slippery Slope: The Slippery Slope is a type of non sequitur in which if p occurs, then q will occur, followed by r, s, t, and the rest. For example, one Slippery Slope often used is that if gay people are allowed to marry then straight marriages will fall apart, families will dissolve, child abuse will grow common, dogs will marry cats, the continents will fall into the sea, we'll all drown and on and on. Some of these non sequiturs are actually logical when isolated. If marriages fall apart, families will dissolve. If continents fall into the sea, we'll drown. However, these few logical pairs are captured within an imagined chain reaction that makes little sense.

6. The Straw Man: The Straw Man consists of arguing something other than what is actually stated. For example, imagine I stated that I did not believe that Wicca was whatever anyone said it was, and that there were some objective qualities of "Wiccanness." A Straw Man response to this would be that I thought that Wicca was only what I said it was and how wrong such a view would be. In fact, my statement, that there were objective qualities are the very opposite of "what I said it was." This can be a hard to understand thing. Imagine, instead, a regular fight I have with my son. One of his chores is to do the dishes. He has to do them every day. One of his arguments is that I want him to spend *all his time* doing the dishes, and that he has other important things to do. This *all my time* argument is a Straw Man. If I wanted him to spend *all his time* doing something, he'd have every right to object, but in reality, I want him to spend a small percentage of his time doing something.

7. The Red Herring: Both The Red Herring and The Straw Man share a common goal: they divert people from the actual discussion at hand. In The Straw Man, the diversion is in the form of arguing against something, and in the Red Herring, the technique is to bring something up with little or no relationship to the topic at hand with the goal of diversion. Using the 1x3=4 example, a Red Herring might work like this:

Joe: 1x3=4
Mary: No, 1x3=3!
Joe: Numbers are given too much stress in our society; we should focus on communication skills instead. Did you know that over 50% of college freshmen need some kind of remedial education? Doesn't that disgust you?
Mary: That's horrible! My brother needed to take reading in college, even though he'd placed out of it in 9th grade...

As you can see, if Joe then proceeded to argue against numbers, as if Mary had made a statement regarding them, he could turn his Red Herring into a Straw Man, but instead, he starts a whole new conversation. This is the difficult-to-understand difference between the two.

8. Ad Hominem: The Ad Hominem is an attack based on the author of the comment. "Of course you object; you're a girl!" is a good example. Wiccans get this a lot from proselytes, who respond to being told to move along with "Of course you can't see the truth! You're deluded by Satan!" In short, an Ad Hominem is a statement that the person with an opinion is not entitled to that opinion, or is to be automatically disregarded, on the basis of who or what that person is.

9. The Bandwagon: The Bandwagon uses peer pressure to make a point: All the cool teens love CheesyChips! If you hate CheesyChips, you're a loser! This is actually shockingly common in Wiccan literature, where you sometimes come upon people who will outright state that if people object to them they aren't "real Wiccans."

10. Poisoning The Well: Poisoning The Well is similar to the Ad Hominem and sometimes takes the same form. It is the attempt to stifle debate by painting the other side of a debate as automatically wrong. This comes in two forms, the first is similar to guilt by association, in which a person claims that those who disagree with him are somehow bad and wrong and therefore if you disagree you are bad and wrong as well. The second form is disregarding something said on the basis of a claim about that person, similar to Ad Hominem, but going a little further... if they object to it, it must be good! A common target is televangelists. Such people regularly say things that are completely wrong, but every now and then they get something right. So, if you are told that a televangelist says that 1x3=3, a Poisoning-the-Well fallacy would be that 1x3=3 *must* be wrong because it was said by a televangelist. In short, it's constructing an argument so that the next person who comes to it (like the next visitor to the well) is affected by it.

All of these logical fallacies can be used both consciously and unconsciously, and examining them in your own thought processes can be very enlightening. When noticing them, however, it's good to keep in mind that not all logical fallacies are the result of someone trying to get one over on you. Often people think they are being quite logical even as they are not.

Exercise:

To show how this is relevant to the discussion of Wicca, and how important knowing these fallacies is, I've gleaned two paragraphs from the web by doing a websearch, finding two sites that said the same thing, and coming up with a third version of the materials, in my own words. For exercise, I'd like you to find the logical fallacies in these paragraphs. Every sentence contains at least one fallacy, and all ten are represented in the passage.

> *Wicca is the ancient religion of the Paleolithic peoples. We know this because of the cave paintings they made to describe their religious ceremonies. The paintings of men with antlers and herds of deer represent the horned god and the mother goddess of the animals. The mother goddess is a goddess of love who cares for all things in the world and they love her in return. We must be thankful to her everyday for the life that springs from her because otherwise we'd be dead. Her love is as old as the stars and so is her religion. Those who object to her religion just do not know her love. Many of them are really Christians who hold onto their old religion.*

> *Many people object to the idea of Wicca as an ancient religion because they believe that there is not enough evidence simply because they don't see it. These people are not well respected by their peers. They believe we should take out the things that reference it, but if we do that, what comes next? First we lose anything that is not agreed upon by the elite Wiccan snobs, the history goes, then the gods, then the rituals themselves until we don't have any Wicca anymore. These people want us to give up Wicca and follow their new religion. They teach that we are totally wrong and misguided but we know who the real misguided people are, don't we?*

Appendix D: Creation Myths, Ancient and Modern

When I wrote, in *Wicca 333* that any discomfort we felt at hearing The Big Bang described as a myth was something we needed to reconcile at a personal level, it was the type of statement a teacher makes in the hopes that some bright star will question them upon it. While only two people to date have questioned me regarding it, I hope that it made a twinge in some of you, and hope that it made you rethink some of your ideas.

Why? Well, what is a myth? As we discussed in *Wicca 333*, a myth is more than a story told as true but later proven to be false or a lie. While our modern culture sometimes uses the word in that way, the core of the word comes from the same Greek word used for any story. That's what a myth is, a story.

Stories can be fiction or non-fiction, true or false. A story can give us information ("Today I saw a story on the news...") or a story can make us feel a certain way. The term story, like the term myth, says nothing about the truth or lack of truth of the story, nor whether it is fictional or non-fictional. All it says is that it is a story, and it serves the purpose that a story does.

So, what is the purpose of a creation myth, the type of myth that I assigned to The Big Bang? The purpose of a creation myth is to explain how we got to this point in time, either as humans in general (for example in the myths of Adam and Eve or evolution), or the Universe as a whole. In general, a creation myth teaches using the common science of the day, which may be nothing more than superstition. Also, however, when dealing with the present day, they may use real hard core valid scientific thought.

It is, however, still a story... a myth... an explanation of perceived phenomena. This simple fact, however, bugs us. We have been indoctrinated by our cultures to hear "myth" and think false. We hear the word myth and we contrast it with the terms we use of our own stories. We call our stories science, religion and news and those of others myths, legends and stories.

When we have this prejudice — for that's what it is — we cannot objectively study creation myths. We have to first set aside those notions of the other as lesser before we can even look at the myths. Once we've done that we can object or agree with creation myths freely, but we must not object to them just because they aren't our myths.

So the challenging language defies us not to think of The Big Bang as a lesser creation myth, but to associate any problems we have with other creation myths with their content, not with their status as the myths of a sort of nebulous "them." We cannot approach mythology comparatively if "us" and "them" define right and wrong.